THE PLAYS OF S

THE PLAYS OF SAUNDERS LEWIS

Also translated by Joseph P. Clancy:

VOLUME I

THE VOW
(Amlyn ac Amig)
THE WOMAN MADE OF FLOWERS
(Blodeuwedd)
THE KING OF ENGLAND'S DAUGHTER
(Siwan)

VOLUME II

HAVE A CIGARETTE?
(Gymerwch Chi Sigarét? 1955)
TREASON
(Brad, 1958)
ESTHER
(1959)

in preparation:

VOLUME IV

THE DAUGHTER OF GWERN HYWEL
(Merch Gwern Hywel, 1964)
THE CONDEMNED CELL
(Cell y Grog, 1975)
THE TWO MARRIAGES OF ANN THOMAS
(Dwy Briodas Ann, 1973)

THE PLAYS
OF
SAUNDERS LEWIS

TRANSLATED FROM THE WELSH BY
JOSEPH P. CLANCY

VOLUME III

Christopher Davies

'Excelsior' first published 1980 in Welsh
by Christopher Davies (Publishers) Ltd.
Copyright © Saunders Lewis 1980
The Translation Copyright © Joseph P. Clancy 1985

'Academic Affairs' first published 1968 in Welsh as
'Problemau Prifysgol' by Llyfrau'r Dryw (Christopher Davies [Publishers] Ltd.)
Copyright © Saunders Lewis 1968
The Translation Copyright © Joseph P. Clancy 1985

'Tomorrow's Wales' first published 1967 in Welsh as
'Cymru Fydd' by Llyfrau'r Dryw (Christopher Davies [Publishers] Ltd.)
Copyright © Saunders Lewis 1967
The Translation Copyright © Joseph P. Clancy 1985

'On the Train' first published 1965 in Welsh as
'Yn y Trên' by 'Barn' (Christopher Davies [Publishers] Ltd.)
Copyright © Saunders Lewis 1965
The Translation Copyright © Joseph P. Clancy 1985

This edition first published 1985 by
Christopher Davies (Publishers) Ltd.
Rawlings Road, Llandybie
Dyfed, SA18 3YD

ISBN 0 7154 0651 5

*Printed in Wales by
Salesbury Press Ltd.
Llandybie, Dyfed*

Published with the support of the Welsh Arts Council.

Contents

Translator's Preface

Saunders Lewis (b. 1893) is, quite simply, the foremost dramatist to have written in the Welsh language. Indeed, in the absence of a strong native tradition, he may almost be said to have invented a dramatic literature for Welsh-speaking Wales, drawing eclectically upon chiefly European modes, traditional and modern, to create theatrical works of art for a culture that for much of his career had no professional theatre. The reader will find in these volumes an ample selection that shows his diversity and development as a playwright, and his continuing exploration of the conditions and consequences of choice, the tensions between *eros* and *agape*, and what William James called "the will to believe".

But these translations are intended not simply to be read, but to provide scripts for theatrical production, for the English-language audiences of Wales and elsewhere, not least my own United States. I have therefore been particularly conscious of Saunders Lewis' own statement that "audible rhythms and the music of speech are of necessity called for in the theatre", a statement which applies equally to his earlier plays in verse, the often heightened prose of his plays of the 1950s, and the more colloquial prose of the later works. I have tried in style to be both faithful to each of the original works and accessible, without excessive Americanisms, to audiences on both sides of the Atlantic. In a very few instances I have dropped or transmuted expressions or allusions incomprehensible to a Welshless audience.

The plays set in the Wales of the 1960s pose special problems, or so at least it seems to a non-Welsh translator, because of the nation's modern bi-lingualism. Must these characters be presented as speaking the English they would also use every day, or may the translator, while trying to avoid the effect of "quaintness" that has often afflicted efforts to suggest Welsh-speakers, allow them some phrasings and rhythms they would probably not carry over to their English speech? In this respect, as several readers of my typescript have noted, these translations in particular need to be tested by actors and directors. So also with my use or omission of contractions in these and the other plays: I have tended to avoid contracting when I could "hear" options I believed should be left open for the actors speaking the lines — even at the risk of having the reader occasionally find the dialogue a bit stiff. I hope indeed that all the scripts will have the benefit of more exploration in performance than I have so far been able to give them, and that whatever modifications prove useful may be incorporated in a subsequent edition.

Three of the plays were originally written for radio — two of these I have adapted for the theatre, and the third can be readily adapted by various means. One play written expressly for television had already been adapted to the stage by the playwright; a second is suited to staging without any modification. I have included, for reasons given in my prefatory notes to the work, a translation of the short novel *Merch Gwern Hywel* in Volume IV.

Prefatory notes to the plays have been chiefly designed to give a basis for programme notes rather than to offer critical analysis. I have not translated Saunders Lewis' own prefaces to various plays, since these often deal with matters of concern chiefly to Welsh-language readers at the time of the play's publication, but I have quoted from them when it seemed advisable. While I have added some information for readers when I thought it might be useful, I have been mindful that this cannot be consulted by a theatre audience and tried to keep it to a minimum.

Although I had thought in planning this book to write a full-length critical introduction, it now seems to me preferable to allow the plays to make their impact without the potential distractions of critical intervention, while giving assistance on what C. S. Lewis called "unshared backgrounds" through the prefatory notes. Readers who wish to obtain an ample view of Saunders Lewis as political theorist and activist as well as man of letters should consult *Presenting Saunders Lewis,* edited by Alun R. Jones and Gwyn Thomas, an admirable selection from his work in many genres (including earlier translations of three plays) together with critical essays on his thought and work, and the excellent monograph by Bruce Griffiths in the *Writers of Wales* series, both published by the University of Wales Press at Cardiff.

What Saunders Lewis' plays most need now, in common with much of the European, British, and American drama of the middle decades of this century, is to be regularly experienced and evaluated in the theatre, and in other countries and languages as well as in Welsh and in Wales. Although he once wrote that "the Welsh are my audience, I have sought no other", it was with Saunders Lewis' consent and encouragement that I undertook these translations, and it is my hope that they will assist in gaining for his plays a lasting international audience.

*   *   *   *

I must thank my college, Marymount Manhattan, for the senior fellowship that allowed me to initiate this work with a stay in Cardiff during Spring 1976. For their kindness and hospitality during that time, I am grateful to Glenys and John Ormond, and to Professor Gwyn Jones and the University College of Wales, Cardiff. Professor R. M. Jones of the University College of Wales, Aberystwyth, has been warmly encouraging and shrewd in advising through the various disruptions and discouragements of these years. Patricia Falkenhain and Robert Gerringer, my ideal American Siwan and Llywelyn, have read several scripts in progress and offered professional advice, as has Diana Lawrence, my ideal American Blodeuwedd. My wife, as ever, has been a challenging and sympathetic reader, and my unfailing support and comfort.

To Saunders Lewis himself these volumes are dedicated, in tribute to a lifetime of heroic choices.

EXCELSIOR

(1962)

When *Cymru Fydd* (the play I have translated as *Tomorrow's Wales*) was published in 1967, Saunders Lewis noted in his preface that this was the third drama in which he had dealt with the contemporary Welsh scene, what he called elsewhere "the crisis of Wales". The previous two were *Excelsior*, telecast in 1962 but because of threats of a libel suit not repeated, staged, or published until Mr Lewis decided to publish the version he had prepared for the theatre in 1979, and *Problemau Prifysgol* (here translated as *Academic Affairs*), written in 1962 but neither staged nor telecast before its publication in 1968. Mr Lewis stated that he regarded these plays as "a triad", and added that "my wish would be to publish them together if it were practical." I have honoured that wish.

The three plays, although unconnected in story and in the three disparate genres of satire, farce, and tragedy, illuminate each other and their period, but it may be too much to hope that they will ever be produced as, say, "A Welsh Triad", in the fashion of such works as Preston Jones' *A Texas Trilogy*. We are now sufficiently distant from the 1960s to begin to see those years as part of "our past", a distinctive historical moment in Wales and the civilization of the West, and I think that any effective production of the plays must now stress this rather than set them in "the present".

For the non-Welsh reader in particular, experiencing the plays as a sequence is a way to acquire some degree of familiarity with their social and political (and, ultimately, religious) context. Saunders Lewis put this "crisis of Wales" into a wider perspective, making explicit what is implicit in the plays themselves, in an article published in 1965; the following excerpt may be useful to the reader and as a quotation for program notes to one or all of these plays:

> What [the majority of Welsh-language authors since 1930]
> have in common is an awareness that the Welsh nation may be
> dying of indifference and sloth and that a literature of a
> thousand years may end with a whimper.
>
> In that they have, as it were, an epitome of what now
> overhangs all Europe, of what threatens humanity, a destruc-
> tion of civilization through apathy.
>
> There is no longer any faith that makes the deferment of the
> nuclear war very urgent. So that a particular Welsh experience
> of this century, the crisis that the Welsh Nationalist Party
> evokes and was organized to avert, takes on universal reference
> and significance. Civilization must be more than an abstraction.
> It must have a local habitation and a name. Here, its name is
> Wales.
>
> "Welsh Literature and Nationalism",
> *Western Mail, 13 March 1965*

Readers and audiences who respond immediately to this "universal reference and significance" may feel no great need to be further informed on Welsh nationalism, and certainly Hugh Hughes in *Excelsior* is as instantly recognizable a figure in politics as Molière's *Tartuffe* is in religious life. The following notes may nonetheless be of help with particular references in this play and the two that follow.

The Act of Union of 1536 decreed that Wales, conquered by England in 1282, should henceforth be "incorporated, united, and annexed" to England. It abolished Welsh laws, outlawed the Welsh language for public affairs, and divided Wales into counties with seats in the English parliament.

The movement of 1894-6 called *Cymru Fydd* (literally "The Wales To Be", often translated as "Young Wales" and translated in my script as "Tomorrow's Wales") had as its central aim the achieve-ment for Wales not of total independence but of Home Rule through its own parliament. It was the first movement to assert that political nationalism was essential for the survival of the cultural nationalism that flourished, under such Welsh Liberal leaders as Tom Ellis and "Mabon" (William Abraham), at the end of the last century and the beginning of this, through such means as the National Eisteddfod (the yearly Welsh-language festival of poetry and song), the annual gathering for communal hymn-singing known as the *gymanfa ganu* (which is still in the United States a major event for Welsh-Americans), and the establishment of the University of Wales, the

National Museum, and the National Library, a cultural nationalism of which the Non-Conformist chapel was the social and cultural as well as the religious centre. *Hen Wlad Fy Nhadau* ("Land of My Fathers"), the composition by Evan and James James written in 1856 and adopted as the Welsh national anthem in 1899, reflects this cultural rather than political nationalism in its celebration of poets and singers, and its prayer that "the old language" will endure.

For a variety of reasons, *Cymru Fydd* collapsed, but the questions it raised did not vanish with it. Writing in 1972, the historian Kenneth O. Morgan stated that

> In the 1970s, as in the 1870s, Welsh politicians are (or at least, ought to be) preoccupied with their countrymen's ambivalent relationship with their English neighbour. While remaining a source of jobs and of investment, England continually threatens to engulf what remains of the native culture of Wales, as it has long since undermined its social structure. The very achievement of Welsh politicians, Liberal and Labour, in winning recognition and equality for themselves and their nation in the wider political unit of which Wales forms a part has simply made the issue more acute . . . the essential difficulty of defining the Welsh political presence, of ensuring that Wales is recognised as a distinct unit, more than a region, yet less than a sovereign state, still remains undiminished. The problem of our 'special relationship' with England is still with us, as it was with our great-grandparents.
> "Welsh Politics", in R. Brinley Jones ed., *Anatomy of Wales*

Plaid Cymru, the Welsh Nationalist Party, was formed in 1925 to sustain the Welsh language and Welsh culture through the achievement of Welsh self-government. Saunders Lewis as a founding member was the first president and a major spokesman for the party during the 1930s. Whatever one's views of this or similar movements elsewhere, some of Saunders Lewis' statements during the 1930s and 1940s serve to distinguish this form of nationalism from others and to relate it to lasting and currently globular questions of cultural heterogeneity and the homogenizing tendencies of "statism", past or present, with its identification of unity and uniformity:

> What then is our nationalism? It is this: to return to the principle [of "one law and one civilization" but with "varied forms and many different hues"] accepted in the Middle Ages;

14

to repudiate the idea of political uniformity, and to expose its ill-effects; to plead therefore for the principle of unity and diversity. To fight not for Welsh independence, but for the civilization of Wales.

*　　　*　　　*

A nation's civilization is rich and complex simply because it is a community of communities, and for that reason also the freedom of the individual is a feasible proposition . . . His liberty depends on his being a member not of one association but of many.

*　　　*　　　*

It is not the function of a country's government to create an integrated system and an economic machinery for the people to accept and conform to. The task of government is actively to create and sustain the conditions which will provide an opportunity, a lead and an encouragement for the nation itself to develop that system which will be a means of securing the welfare of society and the happiness of individuals.

*　　　*　　　*

In their eagerness to be "progessive", they [Welsh religious and cultural leaders] chase after scientistic notions and tendencies which destroy the bases of their own community and of their country's traditions. It is an inability to think that is destroying Wales today. It is for this reason that it is unable to face the tendencies of its age, to comprehend them, and either to accept them boldly with their anti-Christian, Marxist premises, or else to firmly reject them and cast its lot, whether that be right or no, with the traditions of the Welsh forefathers.

*　　　*　　　*

. . . if a nation that has lost its political machinery becomes content to express its nationality thenceforeward only in the sphere of literature and the arts, then that literature and those arts will very quickly become provincial and unimportant, mere echoes of the ideas and artistic movements of the neighbouring and dominating nation. If [the Welsh people] decide that the literary revival shall not broaden out into political and economic life and the whole of Welsh life, then inevitably Welsh literature in our generation will cease to be vital and valuable.

When the Conservative Party ("Tories") was in power in 1951, it established a ministry for Welsh affairs. Creating a Secretary of State for Wales was part of the Labour Party's platform in the early 1960s, and the office was established after Labour won the general election in 1964.

The television programme *Coronation Street*, referred to in *Excelsior*, is a long-running English "soap-opera". Welsh-language broadcasting on radio and television was available for only a few hours a week before Welsh-medium radio began in the late 1970s and a primarily Welsh-medium television channel was opened in 1982, after two decades of intense controversy.

CHARACTERS

Hugh Hughes, a Member of Parliament for the Labour Party
Maggie, his wife
Dot, his daughter
The Reverend Christmas Jones, a young clergyman
Dic Sarc

The action takes place during one evening in the comfortably furnished flat of the Hughes family in London. Acts I and II are set in the parlour room of the flat; Act III in the room Hugh Hughes employs as an office.

ACT I

Maggie Hughes is on the sofa in the parlour, and Dot, in expensively bohemian jeans and silk jumper, stands leaning against the doorpost.

DOT: Oh Mam!

MAGGIE: Hello, Dot.

DOT: Oh, Mam dear!

MAGGIE: Yes, and so?

DOT: Oh Mam!

MAGGIE: I've never denied it.

DOT: *(Moving slowly into the room as though in a dream)* I'm helpless! . . . *(She dances a step or two)* . . . I'm drunk, Mam! I'm reeling!

MAGGIE: *(Quite calm)* Cheers.

DOT: Have you ever been drunk?

MAGGIE: Perhaps, long ago, by accident.

DOT: I don't believe it! . . . *(Another little dance)* I'm drunk now. Not by accident! Tremendously drunk on new wine!

MAGGIE: What did you have?

DOT: An address! A speech! Eloquent, bold, brave, masterful! A call to Wales! A vision!

MAGGIE: Strong drink.

DOT: The cream of eloquence! The best political address I've ever heard! Really, I tell you, really, an inspired speech.

MAGGIE: Has he asked you to marry him?

DOT: That's too bad of you, Mam. It was a political address!

MAGGIE: Of course it was a political address. That's how I married your father.

DOT: Daddy? Oh dear, dear, dear Mam! This was totally different.

17

MAGGIE:	*(Dryly)* At that time, your father was also totally different.
DOT:	There's no possible comparison, Mam.
MAGGIE:	No, I know . . . not yet.
DOT:	To be fair to Daddy, he doesn't pretend that the House of Commons is anything but a business; a matter of bread and cheese.
MAGGIE:	Did he tell you that?
DOT:	Daddy doesn't practise hypocrisy, except when he has to on the stage of the National Eisteddfod on the Thursday afternoon. That's why I have so much respect for him.
MAGGIE:	It's just as well you have respect for him. You're very much alike.
DOT:	Don't throw cold water on my drunkenness. Politics has turned into a vision for me tonight. I saw Wales, Mam! Wales!
MAGGIE:	Oho! Nationalism?
DOT:	Plaid Ymreolaeth Cymru: The Party for Welsh Self-Government. Have you heard of them?
MAGGIE:	They've been at it for some years now.
DOT:	Maybe so. I didn't take any notice until tonight. Until I went to hear Chris.
MAGGIE:	Chris? Who is Chris?
DOT:	Oh Mam, the minister. The Reverend Christmas Jones.
MAGGIE:	Good Lord! Chris! . . . The minister!
DOT:	Mam dear, don't be so dreadfully old-fashioned! Sometimes a person would think you've never been outside a village in Wales!
MAGGIE:	It's true enough. I haven't.
DOT:	There's only five years difference in age between Chris and me.
MAGGIE:	Is there anything else between you?
DOT:	Yes. The enthusiasm of tonight's meeting. He's coming here to have supper with us. He won't be long. I just wish you'd heard him.
MAGGIE:	I hear him twice a month, preaching.
DOT:	I know. It's not at all the same thing.
MAGGIE:	He's a good preacher.

DOT: There's no denying that, but no one can say anything new in a sermon.

MAGGIE: The worst of it is that so many try.

DOT: There were about forty of us London Welsh at the meeting tonight, and many born in London like me. But, believe me, after Chris spoke we all had *hiraeth* for Wales, a yearning to go back to the old country and work for it and give ourselves to it. Can you understand that?

MAGGIE: Adolescent rock and roll.

DOT: I'm twenty-one.

MAGGIE: And not sobered-up.

DOT: Don't you believe me?

MAGGIE: *(Quite sharp)* My dear girl, I'd like you to be so sure of yourself that you don't care a button whether I believe you or not.

DOT: It's a new experience for me.

MAGGIE: You've been in Wales every summer holidays and at the Eisteddfod.

DOT: That was Daddy's business! Shepherding the constituency.

MAGGIE: I taught you Welsh.

DOT: For the chapel!

MAGGIE: No . . . For myself, so I wouldn't be a foreigner in my home as well as on the streets of London.

DOT: I never thought about Wales having a claim on me until tonight.

MAGGIE: And now?

DOT: Now I have an aim, a purpose in life.

MAGGIE: Of course. He's coming here for supper?

DOT: Coming here? . . . Oh! Chris? . . . Yes, I asked him.

MAGGIE: Are you going to accept him?

DOT: Accept him?

MAGGIE: You know what I mean. Do you intend to marry him?

DOT: *(With a cry)* Mam, why are you so cruel?

MAGGIE: I didn't mean to be.

DOT: It's a cruel thing to read people's minds.

MAGGIE: No, I didn't read your mind.

DOT: Yes, you did.

MAGGIE: I can't read my own mind. I never could.

DOT: Because you're so busy reading Daddy's and mine. All the time, all the time. A gift that belongs to people who have turned sour.

MAGGIE: Who's cruel now?

DOT: Is the truth cruel?

MAGGIE: The truth is the only thing that's cruel. But I wasn't reading your mind this time, only remembering.

DOT: Remembering what?

MAGGIE: Remembering coming home from a meeting of Cymru Fydd twenty-four years ago, on a moonlit night in the country.

DOT: Cymru Fydd?

MAGGIE: Tomorrow's Wales, a movement for Welsh self-government when I was a girl.

DOT: I see. And Daddy gave an address?

MAGGIE: A young lad, an attorney.

DOT: Was he good?

MAGGIE: I believed he was serious. That proves I too was drunk.

DOT: What happened?

MAGGIE: You.

DOT: Mam! Me!

MAGGIE: Well, three years later. But your existence was arranged for that night.

DOT: *(Laughing)* And that was the only fruit of the meeting?

MAGGIE: That's the only fruit of every Welsh movement for self-government. They're excellent schools of love.

DOT: Chris is different.

MAGGIE: A minister, not an attorney.

DOT: Chris is in earnest.

MAGGIE: Right. And I shall have a grandchild.

DOT: No, Chris is in earnest about Wales, its mission in the world, the need for a Welsh political movement, for an independent Welsh party in Parliament to argue for the rights of Wales, for self-government for Wales — Oh! . . . Chris!

          (The Reverend Christmas Jones stands in the door. Dot puts her two hands in his and leads him to her mother.)

          . . . Here he is, Mam, the lad who's given me, an M.P.'s daughter, faith in politics!

CHRIS: Good evening, Mrs Hughes.

MAGGIE: How are you, Mr Jones? You had a pretty good meeting?

CHRIS: May I thank you?

MAGGIE: For what?

CHRIS: For not saying "you were inspired"!

MAGGIE: Are you afraid of being hypocritical?

CHRIS: You know, on Sunday evening at the end of service, if a deacon comes up to me and smiles, "Well, you were inspired, Mr Jones", I have all I can do to keep from socking him in the jaw.

(Dot laughs with obvious admiration.)

MAGGIE: You weren't in the pulpit tonight.

CHRIS: I'm not so sure about that. I'm a rather new young minister in London. But without some degree of fanatical patriotism, how can the Welsh-language churches of this city keep going? Welshness is as indispensable as faith if we want Welsh-language churches to continue.

MAGGIE: Then it's London that's made you a nationalist?

CHRIS: No. The divinity college did that. The teacher of church history. You know of him. I heard him talk about Hus defending the independence of Bohemia, about Luther creating the German language and nation! It was impossible for a Welshman to listen to him every week without becoming a nationalist.

MAGGIE: I hadn't thought church history could be so dangerous.

DOT: History *is* dangerous. The people who have forgotten their history are a dying people. Because they have no roots. Right, Chris?

CHRIS: I was lucky. At just the age when a person is most alive to impressions, most ready to accept a conviction that will sustain him for the rest of his life, I had a message, I had a vision, I had a purpose in life.

MAGGIE: And then a call to London.

DOT: But to a Welsh-language church, Mam, our church.

CHRIS: I consider a Welsh-language church in London a part of Wales.

MAGGIE: And I've been here for twenty-two years without shedding my *hiraeth*, a foreigner.

DOT: I was born here. How can I be a foreigner? This is my home.

MAGGIE: A flat! Leased and rented!

DOT: *(Cheerfully)* It's not my fault that my home is a flat. I like the flat.

MAGGIE: The chick who was raised in hell! It's my fault, I know.

CHRIS: I can't see it as a fault!

MAGGIE: Are you from the country too, Mr Jones?

CHRIS: Of course. But I think the children of these big towns strike their roots deeper in their district today than we country children. Here in London they're constantly present in their city, throw their lives into it, know their square mile of streets and shops and people. As for us, the country children, our years pass by in a bus and a train and strange towns. By the time we leave college we don't belong to anywhere. None of our friends are boys and girls from our village. We haven't seen them grow up. We're completely uprooted, and a great many of us have lost our Welsh.

DOT: Chris, that's what you said at the meeting! I knew there was personal experience behind it all, you were so passionate.

MAGGIE: Was coming to London easy for you then?

CHRIS: I obeyed a call, the call of a church. You know what our credo is about a call?

MAGGIE: I can see that accepting a call is a proper thing for the preacher. Not so easy, I suppose, for the nationalist?

CHRIS: At the time, mercifully, I had no choice.

DOT: *(Laughing)* Are you sorry, Mam?

MAGGIE: "Sorry" is not the right word.

CHRIS: What if you had the choice to go back?

MAGGIE: Bless you, my boy, the only pavement in London that brings tears to my eyes is where one takes the train to Wales — Number Two Platform Paddington Station.

DOT: I told Mam that your address tonight aroused a yearning to go back in all of us.

CHRIS: Did you think so? What I was doing was arguing with myself.

22

DOT:	About going back? Why, Chris?
	(A momentary pause)
CHRIS:	This is somewhat confidential, Mrs Hughes.
MAGGIE:	I don't welcome confidences, Mr Jones.
DOT:	*(Angrily)* Mam!
MAGGIE:	My daughter, as you see, is different.
CHRIS:	But I would very much like to have your advice. After all, Mr Hughes is a deacon in the church.
MAGGIE:	I see. You've had a call.
CHRIS:	*(Surprised, and laughing uncomfortably)* Well, really! It's not all that confidential then. How did you hear of it?
MAGGIE:	You need to make a choice?
CHRIS:	*(To Dot)* Yes. A choice.
DOT:	What do you mean, a call?
CHRIS:	A summons to another church.
DOT:	To be its minister?
CHRIS:	Yes.
DOT:	In Wales?
CHRIS:	My old village. The church I was raised in.
MAGGIE:	Is your mother there?
CHRIS:	She and my sister. I haven't had a formal call, only a letter asking if they may put my name before the church.
DOT:	You haven't answered?
CHRIS:	No. I had the letter Tuesday morning.
MAGGIE:	It's Friday today.
CHRIS:	I must send an answer on Monday. They'll have the letter then before the Wednesday night meeting.
MAGGIE:	In a case like this, Mr Jones . . .
CHRIS:	Yes, please, give me your advice.
MAGGIE:	If you have any thought at all about agreeing, the custom is to put the matter before the deacons . . . and ask their opinion.
CHRIS:	You're keeper of the traditions, Mrs Hughes!
MAGGIE:	You can do that Sunday morning after the service.
DOT:	He can ask Daddy tonight.
MAGGIE:	Deacons are people who are easily hurt, especially when some of them are wealthy and important and others less so. The wisest thing would be to tell them all together.
CHRIS:	There speaks a minister's daughter!

MAGGIE:	If you're thinking of agreeing, that is. You can refuse without saying a word to anyone.
DOT:	He can ask for a raise in salary.
MAGGIE:	First you must decide.
CHRIS:	True enough. I must decide. I must choose . . . It's not so easy. I'm being pulled two ways . . .
MAGGIE:	The way of tonight's meeting?
DOT:	But it's scarcely two years since you came to London!
MAGGIE:	True enough. The church here has claims, mind you.
CHRIS:	*(All his attention on Dot)* And . . . it's only six months — *(The telephone rings in another room.)*
MAGGIE:	It's sure to be your father calling from the House of Commons. You're the private secretary, Dot.
DOT:	Oh Mam, won't you go answer it? Chris's news is so sudden, so exciting . . . And there's never any business on a Friday night.
MAGGIE:	*(With a smile, rising and going)* And you want to help him decide. Remember Kipling's warning, Mr Jones, it's easier to go to heaven on your own. *(Exit. Pause.)*
DOT:	What were you going to say, Chris? It's only six months?
CHRIS:	You're right. It's easier to say it without your mother here.
DOT:	I know . . . *(Both laugh)* Say it now.
CHRIS:	It's only six months since I've come to know you.
DOT:	*(Turning playful)* Oh sir, said she, has that anything to do with a call?
CHRIS:	I have a suspicion, *mademoiselle*, that you know the answer.
DOT:	And I have a notion, *signore*, that I would be quite happy to hear it.
CHRIS:	You would think, dear lady, that your minister was rather bold.
DOT:	I have an idea, reverend sir, that I hope my minister will be a bit bold.
CHRIS:	Then what if I said it would not be easy for me to answer a call that would call me away from you?
DOT:	I'm afraid I would have to answer that I've never heard a minister treat a call so sensibly.

24

CHRIS:	It would be dreadful for me to be forced to choose between going back to Wales and you.
DOT:	*(Keeping the conversation playful)* No head deacon ever heard such comforting words.
CHRIS:	Dot, could you possibly consider coming to Wales with me?
DOT:	*(With a curtsey)* Thank you very much, sir, but no, not without a call.
CHRIS:	A call? From the church?
DOT:	From the minister.
CHRIS:	What do you mean?
DOT:	I mean that my minister is rather slow to take me in his arms.
	(He embraces and kisses her.)
CHRIS:	Is that better?
DOT:	A most enjoyable ministry. You were inspired, Mr Jones!
CHRIS:	The text of the call: can you love me, Dot?
DOT:	Can a cat swim?
CHRIS:	Can you marry me?
DOT:	That isn't so easy. We'll have to put our best foot forwards. We'll have to persuade Daddy.
CHRIS:	Will that be difficult?
DOT:	*(In earnest)* Yes. Quite difficult. I'm Daddy's darling. I'm his whole life.
CHRIS:	He has your mother.
DOT:	Mam is his conscience. That's Mam's mistake. A person gets rather tired of his conscience, you know . . . He worships me. It's only with me that Daddy is really in earnest.
CHRIS:	And I worship you too, Dot.
DOT:	Yes, you must.
	(A quick, short kiss, with her hands in his hair)
CHRIS:	. . . That's the nicest thing that's ever happened to me.
DOT:	Kissing?
CHRIS:	With your fingers in my hair.
DOT:	My fingers will be in your hair the rest of your life, my lad.
CHRIS:	Can you face coming back to Wales with me?
DOT:	I knew it was to me you were preaching at the meeting

	tonight. I had a picture of our life together helping to foster a new Wales.
CHRIS:	You're making the choice easier than I'd dreamed. I'm not doing the choosing, you are.
DOT:	And it's you I choose.
CHRIS:	You're willing to have me answer this letter?
DOT:	Where you go, I will go also.
CHRIS:	I'll speak to the deacons Sunday morning.
DOT:	You can speak to Daddy tonight. It's a family matter now.
CHRIS:	You're right, Dot. It's a family matter now. Your family.
DOT:	No, my lad, our family. We'll speak to Daddy together.
CHRIS:	To tell him of both our choices.
DOT:	Our choice of each other and Wales.
CHRIS:	Mind you, Dot, the life of a minister and of a minister's wife in a small country town isn't the same thing as your life here in London.
DOT:	You're right. There are more people in London . . . and more taxis on the street.
CHRIS:	And more streets . . . And a theatre or two, and Covent Garden.
DOT:	Nonsense! They have theatres in Cardiganshire today, and the TV box is as good as a box at the opera.
CHRIS:	It's a thief!
DOT:	Television?
CHRIS:	The incessant English television. "Coronation Street". It gets hold of Welsh-speaking villages and turns them into English villages. The thief must be killed.
DOT:	Who can do it?
CHRIS:	We can, the two of us. Go back to Wales. Resurrect the chapel as a centre of life and energy and joy. Life, real life! Not sitting on a stool watching Englishmen pretending to live.
DOT:	Can you, Chris? . . . Awaken the nation?
CHRIS:	There is no nation. It's necessary to create it, to re-create it. That's our purpose, Dot. That's our call. It's part of our faith. That's the next revival.
DOT:	It isn't too late?
CHRIS:	Have you ever heard of Gruntvig?

DOT:	Gruntvig? . . . From Denmark, wasn't he?
CHRIS:	One of the happiest countries in Europe today. But when Gruntvig was a young man Denmark was as miserable and lethargic and unsure of itself as Welsh-speaking Wales is today. Gruntvig created a Danish nationalist movement, through people's schools, by teaching the common people their ancient history and their ancient songs, by resurrecting a patriotism that had died.
DOT:	Just as you said at the meeting. In your address to *me*.
CHRIS:	Gruntvig was a minister too. I would like to be a Gruntvig for Wales. Stand against the tide and save our nation.
DOT:	You will, Chris, you will! That's your call. You have the gift. It's in your blood. It puts fire in your preaching. And I believe in you. I'll be at your side.
CHRIS:	Not just me, Dot, both of us. This is our call. We'll take a vow of fidelity to the call, the call to my father's church and the call to put the old land on its feet again.
DOT:	Yes, Chris, a vow to keep for the rest of our lives.
CHRIS:	A vow to consecrate our lives.
	(They grasp each other's hands and gaze at each other so intensely that they do not see Hugh Hughes who enters and stands behind them.)
DOT:	Oh Chris!
CHRIS:	Oh Dot!
HUGH:	Oh children!
DOT:	Daddy!
HUGH:	Mr Jones! Mr Christmas Jones! I'm glad to see you! . . . *(The big hand-shake)* . . . I'm delighted that my minister comes to our house like this. You're welcome, Mr Jones, always welcome. The wife there has always been used to the company of preachers. That's her family background. *(An arm around Dot)* . . . Perhaps my private secretary is more accustomed to the company of members of parliament. But of course we're preachers too. Preachers who have had a call, like you, Mr Jones, but to a higher service, perhaps, a costlier service, Mr Jones . . . a more important congregation . . . the parliament of Great Britain, Mr Jones.
CHRIS:	To me, Mr Hughes, Wales —

DOT: *(Interrupting him hurriedly)* You're home early, Daddy.

HUGH: Friday, my lass, Friday. Nothing of importance in the House of Commons, the day of the cranks, you get them in parliament as everywhere, a man with a bee in his bonnet, Wales, just as you said, Mr Jones, or some other private member's bill, you know, a measure to forbid hunting hares on Sunday or to forbid holding a Bingo session at a funeral. The day of the tidbits, you see, with all the sensible members on their way home, even the Liberals. But it's good to have a Friday in Parliament, mind; it's a chance for an occasional member who's not exactly like everyone else, not, you see, all there — oh you get them in the House of Commons sometimes — it's a chance for him to let off steam . . . You know how to succeed in your calling, Mr Jones — You're a young man, the voice of experience can do you some good. In the House of Commons, in the House of Lords, in Lombard Street, in the ministry? Beware of getting the name of being a man with a bee in his bonnet, a man with a single purpose, and one that's wild and unpopular. Walk the main road, the broad road, get known as a man who's on his mark, a sound, moderate man, one who's never extreme, even if he did read Karl Marx in his youth. It's the middle road every time, Mr Jones. That's the road to success. You stand on the threshold of your career. That's the road! Walk it, the only road to promotion in the world and the church. Excelsior!

MAGGIE: *(Who is standing in the doorway listening)* Would you like some cascara, Hugh?

HUGH: Cascara?

MAGGIE: To help you sober up.

HUGH: I've never been more sober, woman, never more sober. Though I have good reason . . . Yes, many a man, even many an M.P., would have lost his head completely. I have a good deal to digest.

MAGGIE: The important news?

HUGH: What?

MAGGIE: You said on the telephone that you have important news?

HUGH: Yes, I said that . . . Yes, important news. Important to you too. But there it is, it can wait its turn. It's necessary to weigh and measure. It's necessary to consider.

CHRIS: If I'm in the way here, Mr Hughes —

HUGH: My dear Mr Christmas Jones, you are my minister, the minister of the church where I am a deacon. It's impossible for you to be in the way, impossible for your presence on my hearth to be inconvenient. I'm an old-fashioned Welshman, you see, Mr Jones, and to me the minister of my church is like one of the family, just like one of the family.

MAGGIE: The minister thinks the same way, Hugh.

HUGH: Thinks the same way how?

MAGGIE: About being one of the family.

HUGH: Very likely. That's right, that's proper. It's part of a minister's job. That's how a young minister learns from his deacons who have more experience, have won their place and their name in the world before getting promotion in the church . . .

DOT: But the news, Daddy?

HUGH: The news, is it? If I hesitated to tell the news, Mr Jones, it was a little bit of shyness, a shred of humility, if you like, that was responsible for the hesitation. And yet, on second thoughts, I don't know of anyone who should hear the news sooner than the minister of the church —

CHRIS: It's news about the church, Mr Hughes?

HUGH: To some extent, Mr Jones, to some extent. It's important to the church. It can affect the future of the church.

MAGGIE: Hurry up and tell us the worst, Hugh.

HUGH: The worst? Yes, that's it, isn't it? But it's even worse that I don't know which is the worst. That's the difficulty, you see. By looking at every side of the problem, the worst can be the best, I suppose.

MAGGIE: Tell me, are you drunk, or am I?

HUGH: That's the problem, it's necessary to make a choice. You see, Mr Jones, a man at my age, and with my experience, and my responsibility, finds himself suddenly, without his ever dreaming of it, in a crisis as it were, between Scylla and Charybdis, if I may borrow a line of poetry for the moment —

29

CHRIS: A well-known reference, Mr Hughes.

HUGH: Yes, isn't it? Though I can't for the life of me remember who the two friends were. But there it is, I'm in a crisis like them. Mr Jones, you're a young man and your way in life is clear and simple. You've never had to face a crossroads in your career. You've never had to stand aside and consider, to choose between two calls, to decide, to change perhaps the whole pattern and direction of your life, to sacrifice everything you're accustomed to. It's a terrible thing to come upon a man suddenly, without warning, Mr Jones, the hour of choice, the hour of choice!

DOT: What is it you must sacrifice, Daddy?

HUGH: Ah! That's the great question! That's the heart of the choice! That's the crossroads! You see, Mr Jones, I've been a member of the House of Commons for eighteen years, the best years of my life, the years of judgment and prudence and maturity. It's true that my party hasn't had a chance to govern this realm, except for one brief period, during that time, and I was a new member then. So unfortunately I haven't had an opportunity to be a member of the Privy Council, a Right Honourable, you know. Well, that's the way things are, and a man is better off not grumbling. Still in all, the House of Commons gets hold of a man, you see. Even a private member is an Honorable Member.

CHRIS: And yours is a very honourable place there, Mr Hughes.

HUGH: You've heard that, Mr Jones? A young minister in London has an opportunity to talk with the Welsh members of Parliament and sometimes hear them address the House. That's a very special advantage, it's an education for a young preacher, isn't it? I've noticed its influence on your preaching: it's broadened your horizons, hasn't it? Expanded your mind? Yes, I myself have had the opportunity to rivet the attention of the House, with the whole Cabinet on the bench in front of me, listening intently, like deacons at the big meetings. That's the reason it's so hard for me to decide which road I should take today.

DOT: Decide what? To leave the House of Commons?

HUGH: That's the problem. That's the choice. To leave the House? Where I have a name, a name such that when it is posted on the wall of the smoking room that I'm to speak, makes them put out their cigarettes to come hear me. Is it my duty? Is this the way I can serve my country? How is the call to be answered?

CHRIS: *(Excitedly)* A call, Mr Hughes? It came to you too? . . . It's like a vision, isn't it? You've heard the call too?

HUGH: Yes, indeed, and well might you say that it's like a vision. It may be a call to higher service, I don't know.

CHRIS: That's what it is, Mr Hughes. Don't hesitate, that's what it is. Higher service.

HUGH: Perhaps. I don't know. I asked for a day or two to weigh and measure. I must reckon the cost, the financial cost, the cost to my career, the cost to my hopes, to say nothing of comfort. But after all, I suppose I should put the call of my country before personal ambition?

CHRIS: *(Grasping Hugh's hand warmly)* Exactly what Dot and I were talking about, Mr Hughes, just now. I didn't dream that you would also have it weighing on your conscience. Because that's what it is, a matter of conscience, your country's call.

HUGH: Just so, my boy. It's this country, isn't it? It has a grip on us, it has a claim. That's what patriotism is. The essence of patriotism, you see, is self-sacrifice. It's necessary to sacrifice a bit of ambition for the sake of what's truly important. I learned that after my first election as a member of parliament. But, believe you me, it's not an easy thing to say goodbye to the House of Commons at Westminster. Everyone who's experienced it, the close and happy life there, agrees that this is the best club in London. There's such a nice spirit there, what the French call a spree decorpse. The friendship and the private trust in each other overcome all party differences. The ferocious attacks on each other's honesty are only something for the debating chamber, part of the game. No, it's an extremely close society, there's brotherly love among the members of all parties, everyone belongs, everyone takes the same oath, everyone is part of the same

31

family. It's no wonder that members of the House of Commons are even prepared to sacrifice the principles they started out with to keep their seats in the House, as one of the family.

CHRIS: The wonderful and magnificent thing, Mr Hughes, is that you, with all your understanding and knowledge of the House of Commons, are prepared to sacrifice it all to answer your country's call—

HUGH: Ah! . . . my country's call!

CHRIS: *(Intensely fervent, begins to sing the Welsh national anthem:)*

Gwlad, gwlad! Pleidiol wyf i'm gwlad!

MAGGIE: What have they offered you, Hugh? Elevation to the House of Lords?

HUGH: That's it, Maggie dear, you old witch—

MAGGIE: Old bitch you mean.

HUGH: That's exactly it. The Prime Minister is worried that the House of Lords has so few men who can argue strongly on behalf of us, the patriotic and moderate socialists, the men of the middle road. And he has offered to elevate me in the next Honours List, as a life lord. That's the crisis, that's the choice, that's the call. I must decide within two days. It's a hard choice. But you see, he is the Prime Minister of Great Britain, and he is the voice of my country's call . . . What shall I do?

(We hear the sound of a gong from an adjacent room)

MAGGIE: That's a better call! A call to eat . . . Come to supper, my lord . . .

CURTAIN

ACT II

The same room after supper. Maggie, Dot, Chris. Maggie is pouring coffee into cups.

MAGGIE: Milk, Chris?

DOT: *(Kissing her mother on the forehead and taking the cup to give it to Chris)*

Thanks, Mam. You can be an angel sometimes.

(Maggie holds the milk-jug waiting for Chris's answer.)

CHRIS: A spoonful, please, Mrs Hughes.

DOT: *(After serving him)* What shall we do, Mam?

MAGGIE: What shall who do?

DOT: Chris and me. Shall we tell Daddy tonight?

MAGGIE: Tell him what?

DOT: That we're in love. That we've promised to marry each other.

MAGGIE: Why not?

DOT: He can't think about anything but the House of Lords tonight.

MAGGIE: Daughters of lords *do* marry — temporarily — sometimes.

DOT: Daddy isn't a lord yet, Mam. He hasn't decided.

MAGGIE: Really? Why did he go to fetch a cigar?

CHRIS: Would that be an obstacle, Mrs Hughes?

MAGGIE: An obstacle?

CHRIS: To our getting married? Marrying the minister of a small country church? The daughter of a lord?

MAGGIE: You're not serious.

CHRIS: Mrs Hughes, I've never been more serious in my life. I love Dot with all my heart, and she's willing to marry me —

33

DOT: And go to live in Wales.

MAGGIE: When did all this happen?

CHRIS: We've been going together for a while —

MAGGIE: Everyone knows that.

CHRIS: But today, after the meeting, I asked her, never dreaming about the House of Lords.

MAGGIE: It's a hard thing to dream about, the House of Lords.

DOT: Once in a while somebody with that sort of dream ends up in the Old Bailey.

CHRIS: I'm afraid that if Mr Hughes goes to the House of Lords, he'll be unwilling to have a snip of a minister as a son-in-law.

MAGGIE: The minister of a small country church?

CHRIS: Exactly.

MAGGIE: The House of Lords isn't on your programme?

CHRIS: *(Laughing)* The furthest thing from it.

MAGGIE: Or the Old Bailey either?

CHRIS: The Movement for Welsh Self-Government. Nationalism and peace. The only nationalist movement in Europe that rejects all forms of violence. What I want is to give my life to that. The Gospel and Wales. That's my programme in life.

MAGGIE: And Dot's as well?

DOT: Mam, those are the kind of ideals I often heard from you when you'd talk of the history of Ireland.

MAGGIE: And you want to get married and escape to Wales?

DOT: My roots are there too.

MAGGIE: Are you certain?

DOT: As certain as Enoch Powell.

MAGGIE: How long will you be certain?

DOT: *(Grasping Chris's hand)* While there's a church at Kidwelly and the little swallow flies above it.

MAGGIE: Very well. Go now, both of you, before your father comes back from choosing a cigar.

DOT: Go where, Mam?

MAGGIE: To Wales, you said.

CHRIS: Now? Both of us?

MAGGIE: Yes. Go pack. I'll say that you've gone for a stroll. There's a train at one A.M. from Paddington. You'll be in

34

	Carmarthen by nine tomorrow morning. I'll give you the money.
CHRIS:	*(In confusion)* But Mrs Hughes . . . I'm a minister.
MAGGIE:	What's the difference? Even a minister can save his soul.
CHRIS:	*(Laughing)* You're not serious, Mrs Hughes?
MAGGIE:	I've never been more serious in my life.
CHRIS:	There'd be instant scandal. You're teasing us, aren't you, Mrs Hughes?
MAGGIE:	My intention was to help you. I'll give you enough money. There'll never be another chance.
DOT:	Be fair, Mam, Daddy isn't as bad as all that.
MAGGIE:	I haven't said a word about your father. What about you?
DOT:	*(Laughing pleasantly)* I'm not a "City of Destruction" either.
MAGGIE:	Who knows? You're female, and twenty years old.
CHRIS:	*(Enjoying the fun)* If I were to run off with a young girl, and her the daughter of a deacon in my church, and a lord-elect too, the story would be in all the papers and on the television news.
MAGGIE:	Dot has an aunt in Carmarthen. She can go to stay with her. There wouldn't be any trouble.
CHRIS:	Really? When I'm supposed to preach here on Sunday? And what becomes of the call?
MAGGIE:	*(Lightly)* I said you weren't serious.
DOT:	Mam dear, we're seriously planning our lives, and you make fun of us.
MAGGIE:	I pity you.
DOT:	Pity? I've never been as happy as tonight.
	(She grasps Chris and pulls him into a little dance.)
CHRIS:	What is there to pity, Mrs Hughes?
MAGGIE:	Tomorrow. Tomorrow's to be pitied in every life.
DOT:	But, Mam, if you'll help us talk to Daddy, everything will be fine tomorrow.
MAGGIE:	Why do you need help? You're the secretary.
DOT:	It's so hard to interrupt him.
	(Hugh enters, smoking a cigar)
HUGH	Coffee? . . . Absolutely . . . Thanks . . . Dic Sarc was on the telephone, Maggie. Dic Sarc is our general secretary in the Socialist Party, Mr Jones. He has enormous influence.

	everything goes through his hands. A bit of an old boy-friend of the wife here too.
MAGGIE:	Is he coming here?
HUGH:	Later on tonight. He's in a hurry to find out.
MAGGIE:	He doesn't know? He's not as stupid as all that.
HUGH:	How could he know? I don't yet know myself, not for certain. It's necessary to ponder, ponder. Of course, Dic's eager for me to accept the honour as usual, more than usual, he's trembling for fear I'll refuse it.
CHRIS:	Why is that, Mr Hughes?
HUGH:	Oh, he's a Welshman, you see, a warm-hearted, patriotic Welshman, with the good of the old country at heart. Another promotion for a Welshman, that's what he sees. We're long-time partners, Dic and I. Double-L-D University of Wales together, *honoris causa*, Gorsedd of Bards of the Isle of Britain together, *honoris causa*, and now he wants me to precede him into the House of Lords, *honoris causa*. A Welshman, you see, a Welshman to the core, the Welshman in politics. There's nothing like him. As they sing on the rugby field, Halleluia!
CHRIS:	But if it's the honour that's important, Mr Hughes, and you're so fond of the House of Commons, why don't they make you a knight, a Sir, and let you keep your place in the House?
HUGH:	A Sir — . . . *Sir* Hugh Hughes? No, no, my boy, never. Everyone would think I am a Welsh-language professor at one of the university colleges. I must keep my dignity.
DOT:	And decide tonight?
HUGH:	It's a matter of business. There are two years before the next general election. The wheel must turn, I believe. If we get a majority next time, I can hope for four thousand a year by remaining in the House of Commons. After all, there's scarcely any constituency that's completely safe for Labour in England, even in the coal-fields full of Welshmen. But we, the socialist members from Wales, can guarantee that there will be no change in *our* livelihood. I don't go into the House of Lords for less than five thousand. There'll be hard bargaining tonight.
MAGGIE:	Have you chosen your title?

HUGH:	An extremely important question. I've been worrying, considering, pondering. I wouldn't like to lose my name. The English lords still think that someone raised in the country, a Tory, a hunter, a fisherman, Church of England and a place in *Country Life*, that that's what a lord is, and they're proud to take the name of some village or river. But I'm a Welshman, and I've made a name for my name. And since I haven't had a chance to become the Right Honourable Hugh Hughes, M.P., I'm rather of the opinion that The Right Honourable Lord Hugh Hughes would be appropriate. There's power in the repetition, like repeating the last two lines of the hymn after the sermon on Sunday night, Lord Hugh Hughes! ... What's your opinion?
MAGGIE:	It's like the ending of Beethoven's Fifth Symphony.
HUGH:	Really? Lord Hugh Hughes! What do you think, Dot?
DOT:	Won't it frighten the House of Lords?
HUGH:	Fine. It's high time they were frightened. What's your opinion, Mr Christmas Jones?
CHRIS:	I'm glad you won't lose your name, Mr Hughes. It will be easier for us when we print your name in the list of church officers in the annual report.
HUGH:	No no no, Mr Jones. That's not the way at all. There are times, you know, when it pays for a church to be a bit bold, to make a splash. A church must advertise if it's to succeed and prosper, and that's what a church is for, isn't it? Having a Lord's name in the annual report, and sending copies to chapels in the old country, that would be a pretty big help in this cause. Because it's here in London, for young Welshmen who want to get ahead in the world, that's where the future is.
MAGGIE:	Then Dot is the only one who has decided to change her name.
HUGH:	Dot? But there's no need, my girl. The title won't affect the way a daughter is addressed. I'll ask the opinion of the College of Heralds, of course. If I were to become an earl, then you would be addressed differently too. Things can develop, who knows? But not tonight.
MAGGIE:	Dot is eager to change.

37

HUGH:	Good Lord! This isn't the time to change, Dot dear. Do you consider that "Hugh Hughes" is somewhat monotonous or too democratic? But in London it will be "Lord Hugh Hughes", and on the stage of the National Eisteddfod it will be "Yr Arglwydd Huw Huws", to rousing cheers. "There's Miss Hughes, the Lord's daughter" — what could be better?
MAGGIE:	Jones.
HUGH:	Jones? Jones? Impossible! . . .
MAGGIE:	There's more than one Jones
HUGH:	There's never been a Lord John Jones.
MAGGIE:	There's been someone better, — the Reverend John Jones, Talsarn, the great preacher. . . Dot's choice is "Mrs Christmas Jones."
	(Maggie collects the coffee things on the tray and exits.)
HUGH:	Is this true, Dot?
DOT:	It's sure to be, Daddy. Mam's not a member of parliament.
HUGH:	But, my dear child, you can't just go do things like this. It's impossible.
DOT:	I agree, Daddy, utterly impossible. It wasn't my idea. You deacons are the ones responsible.
HUGH:	The deacons?
DOT:	You gave a call to a young unmarried preacher to get ahead in the world in London.
HUGH:	Mr Christmas Jones, I didn't expect a blow like this from my minister.
CHRIS:	Neither did I, Mr Hughes. It's been as sudden as an arrow. Cupid must be a church deacon.
HUGH:	You've asked her to marry you?
CHRIS:	And she has consented. I hope, Mr Hughes, that you'll give our love your blessing.
HUGH:	You asked her before you asked me for her hand?
CHRIS:	Well, by this day and age, that's become old-fashioned, Mr Hughes. She isn't a church. It's necessary to be certain of the girl first, and then ask the parents' permission. That's the custom now.
HUGH:	Young man, I, as you know, am the treasurer of that church.

38

CHRIS: But I can't ask the church, there are so many other young women there.

HUGH: Listen. You see my name every month on your paycheck.

CHRIS: A fine signature, Mr Hughes. It raises my spirits to see it.

HUGH: For the past nine months, since she came back from finishing her education, this girl has been my private secretary for my work in parliament. Her salary costs me more, Mr Jones, than you cost that church.

CHRIS: I can easily believe that, Mr Hughes. I've never thought the church was in danger of being prodigal.

HUGH: The church pays the market price. And I pay the market price for a secretary who can answer my constituents' letters in both languages . . . Now look at her.

CHRIS: It's my heaven to look at her.

HUGH: Have you been in Bond Street, Mr Jones?

CHRIS: Bond Street? Well yes, of course.

HUGH: It's part of my daughter's heaven. Have you ever noticed their prices?

CHRIS: Whose prices?

HUGH: Hats, skirt, jeans, tights, jersey, silk blouse, bolero, petticoat, the whole fal-lal?

CHRIS: I'm a minister, Mr Hughes. They're not in my world.

HUGH: They're part of your heaven. They can cost a thousand pounds a year.

CHRIS: Only, Mr Hughes —

HUGH: Exactly, and I'm only Mr Hughes. How much will she cost when I'm in the House of Lords?

DOT: Daddy, Chris and I haven't talked about financial matters at all yet.

HUGH: No? Was I mistaken? He hasn't asked you to marry him?

DOT: Yes, of course he has.

HUGH: That's a financial matter.

DOT: No, it's proof that he really loves me.

HUGH: He's a minister. He's married more than one young couple himself. He knows that worldly goods are bound into the marriage vow. It's very much a financial matter.

DOT: Not to us. Chris and I have fallen in love.

HUGH: Is that any reason to fall into debt? And to marry you would be to fall into a pit of debt.

DOT:	No. We want to go live in the country, back to Wales.
HUGH:	Who?
DOT:	Chris and I.
HUGH:	In the country ? . . . Farming?
DOT:	Chris has had a call.
CHRIS:	Well, not a formal call. But a letter from my old church, the church I was raised in, asking if I would consider a call to go there as minister.
HUGH:	At what salary?
CHRIS:	The letter didn't mention salary.
HUGH:	I believe you. I know the district, Mr Jones.
DOT:	Dad, don't call him Mr Jones. Call him Chris.
HUGH:	Chris? . . . Why Chris?
DOT:	Because I'm going to marry him.
HUGH:	Nonsense.
DOT:	On my oath.
HUGH:	In spite of me?
DOT:	With your help, Daddy dear. Getting married is a financial matter.
HUGH:	Mr Jones —
DOT:	Chris, Daddy.
HUGH:	Drat you, if I call him Chris, how can I throw him out of the house? . . . Mr Jones —
DOT:	It isn't "Mr Jones" I want to marry.
HUGH:	Who then?
DOT:	Chris.
	(Hugh raises his hand to give her a clout and as she avoids it strikes Chris who cries out.)
HUGH:	Oh! My dear Mr Jones!
DOT:	Chris, Daddy. You can't strike your minister without it being a matter for the society. But you can give a clout to one of the family.
HUGH:	That's what I intended to do. I'm very sorry, Mr . . .
DOT:	There's nothing for it but Chris!
HUGH:	Chris . . . You have a private income?
CHRIS:	Not a red cent, Mr Hughes.
HUGH:	Then how the devil can you talk of retiring?
CHRIS:	Not retiring, Mr Hughes, only accepting a call to a country church in Wales.

HUGH:	Even worse! To live on the dole?
DOT:	Daddy, do you know anything about Gruntvig?
HUGH:	Gruntvig . . . wait now. Yes, tape-recorder and electronics, quite a good company, last year's profits the highest ever. But it's necessary to be careful in putting money into electronics. I have a friend in the House of Commons who knows the market —
CHRIS:	Gruntvig the Danish preacher and nationalist, Mr Hughes. A minister who left the capital to care for a small country church. He established the people's schools of Denmark. He put Denmark back on its feet when it was weakest and the national spirit was at death's door. Dot and I want to try to do similar work in Wales.
HUGH:	Mr Jones —
DOT:	Chris, Daddy, Chris!
HUGH:	Chris . . . I'm a member of parliament and your district is in my constituency. I know every village there. My box in the House of Commons is full of their letters. By voting for me they think they've bought me. There are two things that trouble the country people: can I get a job for their children in London and have I influence to help them in filling out the coupon for the football pools. You talk about reviving country life. There's no country life to be revived. There's no chapel life either. You're living back in the nineteenth century. It's not country life that exists in Wales today — it's a shabby town life gorging on *Coronation Street* and seeing it as heaven.
CHRIS:	But unless a few people take the risk, it will be all up with Welsh-speaking Wales.
HUGH:	*(After a fit of laughter)* Ha ha ha ha! Welsh-speaking Wales! My dear boy, we're not on the stage of the Eisteddfod here.
CHRIS:	But one has to try. What meaning does our life have otherwise? That's why I'm in the ministry. Wales is our responsibility.
HUGH:	Try as much as you like, young man, but leave my daughter in London. Every poet has a right to his poverty, but it's a pretty filthy trick to force poverty on his

	sweetheart. Love is a terribly selfish thing. Believe you me, I've been through the cauldron too.
DOT:	Chris isn't forcing Wales on me, Daddy. It was my choice.
HUGH:	A miserable, bare, monotonous life in a foreign wilderness, — that would be your fate, Dot, as a country minister's wife in Wales. Even for a girl raised in the country it would be hard.
DOT:	Chris told me that himself, but we have plans, experiments.
HUGH:	A revival?
DOT:	Chris sees it as a revival.
CHRIS:	Yes, but a revival that unites religion and politics, that puts a new spirit into the chapel and the nation.
HUGH:	A revival that would antagonize every deacon and deacon's wife in the chapel. There's only one way to keep things bright in the chapels in Wales today, that's to close your eyes and not see that everything's dying. That's the only chance for a country minister to reach his pension.
DOT:	But Chris has a message, a vision, —
HUGH:	And for Ch-ch-chris's sake you're choosing your grave, to die of cold and loneliness within two years.
DOT:	Well, look at him, listen to him. He's so holy and so handsome and his passion is so intense. How could I help it?
HUGH:	You see, my boy? It isn't child's play to ask a young woman who's been gently raised to marry you. To be a revivalist and a married man is not a practical combination in Wales today. Indeed, it's very seldom that the minister of a church has the right to marry. It isn't honest. Look at the ministers of Wales. It's most often the wife who sustains the minister and the minister who sustains the congregation — if there is a congregation. Which is really important to you, your own heaven or leading Wales to the heaven of your dream?
CHRIS:	Don't have any doubts about me, Mr Hughes. The first place in my heart belongs to Dot.
DOT:	Perhaps we weren't very practical, Chris.
CHRIS:	Besides, I haven't had anything like a call. Just an

	unofficial letter that suggested putting my name before . . .

DOT: Mam said that two years is a very short time for a minister to remain in a church in London.

HUGH: There it is. Your mother's a sensible woman, that's my opinion too as a deacon.

DOT: You yourself said, Chris, that a Welsh-language chapel in London is part of Wales just like a chapel on Welsh soil.

HUGH: Very good, my boy. That's the home of the Welsh language. The language of the hearth and the chapel. It's necessary to keep a warm little corner for the Welsh language amid the hurly-burly of important things and the busyness of life. That's the function of the Welsh chapels in this city, to give a refuge to the old tunes and the old hymns. I wouldn't be surprised if some line of Alun Mabon's mightn't be quite appropriate in my first speech in the House of Lords.

CHRIS: And I'm grateful for your advice, Mr Hughes. I'm rather certain now that it's my duty to remain in London.

DOT: That's what you're in favour of too, aren't you, Daddy? Then I can go on working as your private secretary.

HUGH: After you're married?

DOT: Chris and I would have around £1200 in salary then.

HUGH: It isn't enough.

DOT: But you'll be in the government after the next election. And I'll have a higher salary then, without costing you anything.

HUGH: This is the girl you wanted to bury in the country, Ch-ch-chris. Have you ever had an interest in politics?

CHRIS: Of course, Mr Hughes, for years. I was speaking just tonight at a meeting of the Party for Welsh Self-Government, the London branch.

HUGH: Yes, yes, the Welsh language and patriotism and peace throughout the world. That's not what I mean — I mean *politics.* You have a gift for speaking. There's an opportunity for you in politics.

CHRIS: I'm not sure I follow you, Mr Hughes.

HUGH: You're asking a young woman to marry you. Therefore you need to arrange to support her. You haven't any capital to invest. What do you have? A gift for preaching, a characteristic Welsh talent for making speeches. That's capital in itself. That's what brought you here to London. It's worth good money. But it's necessary to invest it wisely, like that steward, "to dig I am not able and to beg I am ashamed." That's the right spirit. And the field for you if you want to marry is politics. That's a safe way to get ahead in the world. Politics and religion, they put money in the purses of Welsh mothers, and once you're elected to parliament for the workers of Wales your future is more secure than the Bank of England.

(The door opens for Maggie and Dic Sarc.)

MAGGIE: Here he is, the devil himself.

DIC: Now then, fair play, Maggie . . . Hello Dot!

MAGGIE: Mr Christmas Jones, our minister; Mr Dic Sarc.

CHRIS: Good evening, Mr Sarc.

DIC: *(shaking hands)* I've heard of you. A fervent speaker! One of these nationalists, aren't you? . . . Well, Hugh old lad, is Maggie furious? I was almost afraid to ring the bell.

MAGGIE: You have the gall to ring any bell. But this time you've won. I hope you've come to confess.

DIC: Confess what?

MAGGIE: Dic was the only one who remembered that it's April first today.

DIC: Maggie!

DOT: April first, April Fool, Daddy!

HUGH: What?

DOT: What?

DOT: The House of Lords! It's Dic Sarc's joke!

HUGH: Dic! Dic Sarc! A hell of a joke! To deceive and make a fool of your oldest friend. There's no way to forgive that sort of injury. It's spitting on trust and friendship, that's what it is. Turning an old friend and an old colleague into a laughing-stock. Raising my hopes to the sky and then dropping them down to the ground the way you'd drop a pair of trousers. It's hard to believe —

DIC: *(After trying several times to stop him, he shouts at the top of his voice:)* Hugh!

44

HUGH:	No!
DIC:	Hugh, you —
HUGH:	My name isn't Hugh You, it's Hugh Hughes, socialist member of parliament and a lifelong enemy to the House of Lords, both lords who inherit and lords who are created. It was for your sake and the sake of the socialist party that I agreed —
CHRIS:	(*Grasping Hugh and facing him*) Mr Hughes, listen! This isn't a joke. And you're not an April fool.
HUGH:	What?
CHRIS:	Listen to him, to Mr Sarc. What he's saying is important.
HUGH:	Is this true, Dic?
DIC:	Of course it's true. That's what —
HUGH:	Why the devil didn't you say so before? Who said it was an April fool trick?
DIC:	Nobody said it. Maggie was voicing her hopes.
HUGH:	Maggie's hope is that I'll lose my seat in both Houses, so that she can return to Wales.
DIC:	Poor Maggie, I know what's bothering her. She's mad as a hornet because within some four months she'll have to answer to the name of Lady Margaret, and she'll be ashamed.
HUGH:	Lady Margaret Hughes! On my life that hadn't entered my mind. But of course, Lord and Lady Hughes.
DOT:	That won't change anything, Daddy. That's what Mam has always been.
MAGGIE:	Hugh hasn't decided anything yet, Dic. He doesn't know whether he can afford it.
DIC:	Have you been trying to prevent him?
MAGGIE:	Those days are long past. You're the only one who remembers them. Hugh got ahead in the world in spite of his wife. He owes nothing to anyone, as it's easy to see.
HUGH:	Dot, take Uncle Dic into the office so that we can talk business. I'll follow you in a minute . . .
DOT:	(*As they go*) And Chris too, I hope.
HUGH:	Chris, my boy, I'll send for you within ten minutes. Think it over seriously . . . politics . . . my daughter's prosperity and happiness are in your hands . . . (*Exit*)

45

MAGGIE:	Are you going to stay, Chris?
CHRIS:	If it's all right with you, Mrs Hughes. That's what Mr Hughes asked me to do and I have to stay to see Dot.
MAGGIE:	You're welcome to stay. But I'd rather see you go.
CHRIS:	I'm sorry. Am I in the way?
MAGGIE:	We're in the way. Myself and my family.
CHRIS:	In my way?
MAGGIE:	It was your way when you came here tonight.
CHRIS:	The way to Dot's heart is my way.
MAGGIE:	It's a dangerous way; there are robbers.
CHRIS:	You helped me. You opened up a way to talk to her father.
MAGGIE:	That was wrong of me. This craving to please is a curse.
CHRIS:	Mrs Hughes, my head is spinning with happiness. I hadn't the least notion that Mr Hughes might bring such news home tonight.
MAGGIE:	Neither did I. It's too bad he's spoiled the evening for you.
CHRIS:	Spoiled the evening! Oh. I see your point. Dot's news and mine is over-shadowed by the news her father had.
MAGGIE:	You see this news as good news?
CHRIS:	The best possible news for Mr Hughes and yourself, but also and especially for Dot.
MAGGIE:	It won't make much of a difference to Dot, I should think. The most important thing for her had happened already.
CHRIS:	And thank heaven for that. Think! If I'd known, I'd never have dared to kiss a lord's daughter.
MAGGIE:	Your humility frightens me. When she comes back the taste of her kiss will be like the ten commandments to you.
CHRIS:	*(After laughing)* I've never been so happy in my life, Mrs Hughes.
MAGGIE:	You're an only son?
CHRIS:	An only child. A proper husband for Dot.
MAGGIE:	And your mother is a widow?
CHRIS:	Yes. She's not in need.
MAGGIE:	She doesn't know anything about Dot?
CHRIS:	Well no, not yet.

MAGGIE: Of course. An only son. A hard letter to write even for a minister.

CHRIS: Yes, it must be written very carefully.

MAGGIE: She knows about your letter from the deacons?

CHRIS: I told her that at once. My letter was somewhat hasty.

MAGGIE: To have you back as minister in the chapel you were raised in will be a foretaste of heaven to your mother.

CHRIS: That's the difficulty, Mrs Hughes. I wrote before I'd considered it enough.

MAGGIE: Before you'd kissed a lord's daughter?

CHRIS: *(Enjoying this and not recognizing irony)* Well yes, but not just that. Before I'd talked things over seriously with Dot and her father.

MAGGIE: A revolutionary conversation. Four hours after your sweeping address to the nationalists? You discovered that it isn't so easy to go back to Wales?

CHRIS: A bit of youthful romanticism, I'm afraid. I'm afraid. It was an impractical dream to think of taking Dot to a small country chapel.

MAGGIE: You're quite right.

CHRIS: You agree then, Mrs Hughes? That buries every doubt.

MAGGIE: You'll remain a minister in London?

CHRIS: That is my hope. I can serve Wales the same way here. Dot and I haven't changed our ideas at all.

MAGGIE: You'll remain a preacher?

CHRIS: What else could I be?

MAGGIE: I don't know, — unless a member of parliament.

CHRIS: It isn't through parliament that salvation will come to Wales.

MAGGIE: It raises my spirits to hear you speak the truth.

CHRIS: I must confess, Mrs Hughes, that telling Mam I can't accept the deacons' offer will be a disappointment and a shock to her.

MAGGIE: And telling her about Dot at the same time. That's what will tangle things up from the start, before they've even seen each other. Things will never become easier later.

CHRIS: If only I hadn't been so enthusiastic in telling her in my first letter . . . What shall I do? Give me your advice.

MAGGIE: Run away.

CHRIS: Run away? . . . From whom?

MAGGIE: To your mother. Tonight. Now. You'll be with her by morning. Because she has you there, when you've come for the one purpose of telling her about Dot, the daughter of a deacon in your church, your mother will understand and forgive. And she'll invite her to visit her. Tell her that I'll come too, an old-fashioned Welshwoman, to see her and make her acquaintance.

CHRIS: Mrs Hughes, your advice opens up a path of salvation. That's the way to get Mam to accept Dot. Yes indeed. I'll arrange it with Dot next week.

MAGGIE: Next week will be too late.

CHRIS: But I have to make arrangements with Dot.

MAGGIE: *(After a short laugh)* Yes, I suppose so. Chris dear, it's all up with you. I won't see your mother. And you're the one who said just now that salvation will never come to Wales through the English parliament.

CHRIS: *(nervously, frightened)* You're not well, Mrs Hughes. Your mind is confused. I'm not surprised. Mr Sarc's news is enough to upset anyone. I have some aspirin tablets here. I always carry them in my waistcoat pocket. They're a great help before preaching. Will you take a tablet?

MAGGIE: My sermon is over and I'm terribly healthy —

CHRIS: Oh, no, indeed. May I fetch Dot to help you to your bed?

MAGGIE: Dot isn't aiming for my bed. And here's the proof.
(Dot enters dancing towards Chris and pulls his head down to kiss him.)

DOT: Can you dance, Chris?

CHRIS: Not since the divinity college.

DOT: You'll have to learn again. Every member of parliament under forty dances in some fashion . . . *(and she pulls him into a little dance)* Oh Chris, everything is all right . . . Daddy has accepted you as a son.

CHRIS: He's willing to have us marry?

DOT: He's the one who's opening the way. Making it possible. He's making plans for the wedding. You are his heir and

the wedding must be worthy of a lord . . . Come on, he's calling for you.
(And out they go without looking at Maggie. She watches them and then lifts her arms in a gesture of despair and sinks to her knees.)

CURTAIN

ACT III

A room in the flat that serves as an office for Hugh. Dic Sarc and Dot are there. The time is about ten minutes before the close of Act II.

DIC:	And who is Chris?
DOT:	Our minister. You just met him. Mr Christmas Jones.
DIC:	Oho! Chris! Is he after you —
	(Dot shrugs her shoulders)
	How old is he?
DOT:	Twenty-six.
DIC:	Kissing age.
DOT:	He hasn't strained himself asking for a kiss, Uncle Dic.
DIC:	Did he need to ask?
DOT:	A minister?
DIC:	Some ministers are married.
DOT:	Do I have the look of a minister's wife?
DIC:	You're more like your father than your mother.
DOT:	Daddy enjoys life. And so do I.
DIC:	That's not the way a wife of the manse talks. A member of parliament would suit you better.
DOT:	Of which party?
DIC:	The Tories, I think. They're the English nationalists.
DOT:	You're dreadfully Welsh, Dic.
DIC:	I don't see much harm in that. But why?
DOT:	You haven't been near a chapel for years, but still you set standards for a wife of the manse.
DIC:	I'm not the one who sets them.
DOT:	No? Is there a lady in the case?
DIC:	Your mother was a daughter of the manse.

DOT:	She's still a daughter of the manse.
DIC:	That's my standard.
DOT:	Good heavens! I've never heard you and Mam do anything but bicker with each other.
DIC:	I remember her at your age. She had a walk like Olwen, Maggie Evans of the Manse . . .
DOT:	Uncle Dic! I've never heard this before. Did you lose your heart?
DIC:	I was reading the *Clarion* and Karl Marx and I'd turned my back on the chapel . . . Your father took her.
DOT:	And Mam?
DIC:	Her father was a man from Merionethshire, full of reminiscences about Michael Jones of Bala and Patagonia and Tom Ellis. Your father was also a nationalist at that time, and I was a red-hot socialist. His hero was Mabon with his *gymanfa ganu* and the *eisteddfod*. I didn't have a chance.
DOT:	You're opening my eyes. And the news tonight?
DIC:	Lady Margaret? I don't know whether it's revenge or what. But nobody else has mattered to me.
DOT:	An old bachelor's revenge? . . . Poor Uncle Dic, you'll get a kiss now without asking for it.
	(She puts her arms around his neck and kisses him. Hugh enters.)
DIC:	Well, Hugh. It's all up with you. You can't bargain any more.
	(Dic laughs, Hugh looks at him sharply. Dot places glasses and a jug of water and a bottle of whiskey on the table.)
DOT:	You won't need me, Daddy?
HUGH:	Come back in ten minutes.
	(Exit Dot)
	Why not?
DIC:	I didn't know until Maggie in her usual way suggested it that you were itching to go into the House of Lords. You have to go now.
HUGH:	I have my legal practice here and in my constituency. When the time comes to sell it "Lord Hughes and Co." will raise the price a good deal. But at this time I can't afford it.

DIC: Nonsense, Hugh. You won't be at a loss financially. I've
            looked into the matter carefully.

HUGH: But the Gallup-Poll predicts that we'll win the next
            general election.

DIC: Very well, What of it?

HUGH: What of it? The day of the big prizes. A race for the fat
            posts in a new government.

DIC: But Hugh, you've never learned the job.

HUGH: I have my business in the city every morning. I've never
            had a halfpenny from a labour union except as a fee. An
            independent member, a rare thing in our party, Dic. I
            haven't had the leisure to learn or to shadow a cabinet job.

DIC: Well I know it. Members who are tied to a labour union
            are the chief nuisance of that office of mine. But look here,
            Hugh, you'll have a better chance for a post in the next
            socialist government by going into the House of Lords.
            There's less competition there.

HUGH: But what if we abolish the House of Lords? I've argued
            against the House of Lords all my life.

DIC: Boyo, don't be such an innocent. It isn't through the
            Labour Party that the House of Lords will come to an
            end. We're always a moderate, conservative party in our
            actions; not Bolshies like these Tories. They're so sure of
            themselves they have no respect for institutions or
            traditions. Look at the last ten years! Who but the Tories
            would have dared toss the British Empire to the swine?

HUGH: All right. The House of Lords is to stand. Now, if I go
            there, and if we win the next time, what post will I get? I
            won't go without a promise.

DIC: You know I can't promise anything. I'm not the Prime
            Minister.

HUGH: Your advice will count. Your office guarantees that.
            You're responsible now for moving me into the House of
            Bolshies. I jib if I don't get the promise of a job in the
            government if the chance comes.

DIC: I'm prepared to promise to suggest your name for a post.

HUGH: That's too wide-open. What post?

DIC: That's the difficulty. You haven't specialized. These
            Lords, the ones who go there, are almost all professional

	men, specialists who know their stuff, not a bunch of amateurs in a debating club like the House of Commons.
HUGH:	What post?
DIC:	*(Taking paper and pencil and making a list)* What's in the House of Lords right now? The Overseas Office? Impossible . . . Colonies? It's doubtful that there'll be any left; if there are, thorough knowledge is necessary. Commonwealth Relations? The hardest job of all . . . I'll be hanged, Hugh! I can't think of a single one that suits your talents.
HUGH:	My field is dealing with the moral principles of politics. The tradition of Burke and Engels. There must be a place for that? Government without moral principles is impossible.
DIC:	Yes, yes, they're very valuable for after-dinner speeches. But every job I know of calls for some special technical knowledge, a mastery of background and history . . . Oh, Lord, Hugh! . . . Great heavens!
HUGH:	What is it? You've thought of one?
DIC:	It's made for you. And we both clean forgot about it. Just the post for you. Where there's no end to the need for moral principles. The only post in the government that no one can fill better than you.
HUGH:	Of course! I knew there had to be one like that. Politics hasn't sunk so low that there's no such office. Which one is it?
DIC:	Wales, Hugh *bach!* Wales, land of poets and patriots! Minister of State for Welsh Affairs! We don't dare not fill it. And it must remain in the House of Lords. If it were to go to the Commons the race to grab it would cause a riot. I'd see thirty of the Welsh members rushing in one herd over the precipice to that office of mine.
HUGH:	Minister of State! The Right Honourable Lord! Yes, quite good.
DIC:	Of course, there's one disadvantage. You're a Welsh-speaking Welshman. That might raise a stir.
HUGH:	An accident, Dic, not policy, not at all indispensable for the office.

DIC:	No, no. And in the House of Lords it will be easier to conceal the risk.
HUGH:	There won't be any risk. I'll be careful. It's my experience that there's no prejudice at all against the Welsh language, if we don't force it on the county councils and local government and administrative life. Then there's perfect freedom for the language and everyone who supports it.
DIC:	Exactly, Hugh, that's just the attitude that's necessary towards it in the office.
HUGH:	Moral principles, my boy, I told you there's a place for them. Especially with the county councils. Wales is the paradise of county councils.
DIC:	All right, Hugh, that's it. You can go into the House of Lords with no problems.
HUGH:	No-no-no. Hold on. We've removed one difficulty. But there's another hindrance that's just as great.
DIC:	Another hindrance? . . . Maggie?
HUGH:	No, not Maggie. Maggie doesn't know the difference between the House of Lords and Wormwood Scrubs.
DIC:	Be fair now, there is a difference: you can escape from Wormwood Scrubs . . .
	(Dot comes back in a "Cocktail Party" frock. Dic rises to greet her.)
	. . . Dot, you're like a bolt of lightning. What is it?
DOT:	A new frock . . . *(Turning to show it)* . . . *Chic*?
DIC:	A lady, on my oath. Hugh, this girl could open up a career for a young M.P. if she marries properly. Look at her.
HUGH:	We'll try, Dic, we'll try.
DIC:	No, I'm serious. The appeal of a girl like this is something we can profit by politically. Finding the right M.P. for her, that's the trick.
HUGH:	Now then, Dot, a short memo, please . . . Things are moving. *(Dot sits at the typewriter; Hugh dictates and she types)* . . . A confidential memo in Welsh. That's where the Welsh comes in handy, Dic . . . The Date . . . I agree with the General Secretary to go to the House of Lords on two conditions: first, if we win a majority, I will have the post of Minister . . . in parentheses: Wales. Second —
DIC:	Yes, what's the second condition?

HUGH: My constituency, my lad. You can't expect me to go to the House of Lords and leave my constituency destitute, a prey for any chance newcomer. I have a responsibility to the constituency. I've nursed it, shepherded it, found work for dozens of its children —

DIC: Damn it, Hugh, you're not proposing a toast. Get down to business, please.

HUGH: I must have the choice of my successor. I must have the assistance and blessing of your office to get the local branches to adopt him. Otherwise I'd be betraying the constituency by going to the House of Lords.

DIC: You know that I can't force a candidate on any constituency.

HUGH: I can, if I have your help. You must co-operate to arrange things.

DIC: You have someone already in mind?

HUGH: We can set down a few important principles to start with. First, the next member must be a free man like me, not tied to a labour union.

DIC: I have nothing against that.

HUGH: Second, he must be of the same religious denomination as me. It's a constituency that continues to be very Welsh in spirit, and the ecclesiastical statistics prove that that's totally indispensable.

DIC: Poor Hugh, those religious prejudices are long dead —

HUGH: I'm not talking about religious prejudices. It's a matter of patriotism. Thank goodness that hasn't yet disappeared. The denomination is still the homeland to the Welshman, especially in an election.

DIC: Well, you're the one who knows best about that. I don't mind!

HUGH: Third, — three headings, Dic, as usual, — as you know I've nursed the constituency in moral principles, the precious radical tradition of Welsh non-conformity. I can think of no worthy successor to me but one of the young giants of the Welsh-speaking pulpit.

DIC: Hugh, where is this leading?

HUGH: What?

55

DIC:	When you thresh about with three headings to your nonsense, I know by experience that you have a pretty hard bargain to strike. What is it?
HUGH:	*(Suddenly sitting down)* Marriage.
DIC:	Marriage? You can't!
HUGH:	It's for your sake I'm doing it.
DIC:	It's too late. Maggie wouldn't look at me now.
HUGH:	Not Maggie, you oaf. Her daughter.
DIC:	Dot? No? The little serpent, she didn't say a single word.
HUGH:	You asked for an M.P. as her husband. You insisted you were serious; for the sake of the party. All right, here's your chance. I'm offering you one.
DIC:	That minister in the next room? Dot, is this true?
DOT:	I wouldn't like to contradict Daddy.
DIC:	I'm stupid. I noticed that your eyes were sparkling more than usual. And the very special frock . . . He's a lucky boy, I envy him.
HUGH:	The Reverend Christmas Jones.
DOT:	Uncle Dic, as a favour, I give you the right to call him Chris.
DIC:	He isn't to call me Uncle Dic.
DOT:	But that's what all the members of parliament call you, — and their husbands too!
DIC:	He's not a member of parliament.
DOT:	Dear-dull-Dicky, you're going to lose me if he isn't.
DIC:	An ultimatum, is that it?
DOT:	I gave you a kiss, remember.
DIC:	A kiss of pity.
DOT-	You're under an obligation to me, you old bachelor.
DIC:	He's one of these nationalists, isn't he?
HUGH:	Of course he is. He's in the right tradition. Tom Ellis, Lloyd George, Ramsay Macdonald and I — every one of us was a nationalist to start with. How else does one reach the House of Lords?
DIC:	You want to have him as a candidate to replace you?
HUGH:	That's the second condition in the agreement, Dic.
DIC:	Does he know anything about the policy of the Socialist Party?

HUGH:	Every bit as much as I do.
DIC:	That's what I was afraid of.
HUGH:	He's a nationalist, — someone who's steeped in all the English papers of the Left, with "Land of My Fathers" as a supplement. The radical tradition, boyo.
DIC:	Wouldn't it be better for us to have a chat with him?
HUGH:	Dot, ask the candidate to join us here.
	(Exit Dot)
DIC:	You know, Hugh, when I hear you speak I sometimes wonder whether you're right in the head. But when it comes to bargaining between us, you come out on top every time.
HUGH:	Well, you see, Dic, I never speak without considering things carefully; but when it comes to bargaining between us, I leave everything to my instinct.
DIC:	It was your instinct that brought that minister to meet me tonight?
HUGH:	He was here for supper, and I didn't know any more than you that he was in love with Dot. I never dreamed of him in that connection. A little bit of a preacher, quite an innocent, you know. I can't understand Dot, she's such a clever girl.
DIC:	I'd swear it was all a trick to trap me.
HUGH:	It was after supper I first heard, as I was in the middle of weighing what the House of Lords was worth. I inquired a bit after that. The lad hasn't any money. Well, then you came on the telephone wanting to know whether I'd go to the House of Lords or not. And suddenly everything fitted neatly together. Instinct, you see? Just like Newton and the apple.
DIC:	And Dot is pleased, I think. What will she make of him?
HUGH:	The girl had to have her way. I couldn't reject the boy.
DIC:	The girl has had her share of indulgence, Hugh.
HUGH:	What do you want? A man has to have something besides himself to live for once in a while.
	(Dot and Chris enter hand in hand. Dic rises and shakes Chris's hand.)
DIC:	Congratulations, young man. You know how to choose a wife.

CHRIS: Thank you, Mr Sarc. I hope I'll be worthy of her.

DOT: No more Mister Sarc, Chris. He's been Uncle Dic in this house for as long as I can remember, and that's what he is to you now. When he and I are together without anyone else around, he has a private name, haven't you, Dicky? *(Twining her arm in his)*

DIC: Yes, Dotty.

DOT: And he doesn't always behave like an uncle, Chris. He has a few old bachelor's tricks at times, haven't you?

DIC: It's necessary to please a girl who's been spoiled all her life.

DOT: Now, Uncle Dic, tell Chris what you have to say.

DIC: Your father can explain the matter best. I'll say this much. My friend Hugh here, after years of labour for the Socialist Party in the House of Commons, has been invited to carry on in the House of Lords. Naturally enough he is anxious about his constituency in Wales, the faithful folk. He knows them; and you are also, he says, from the district. So you know that Hugh has always honoured the tradition of the pulpit and the deacon's seat in his political work. He's eager for that tradition to continue. That's the situation, isn't it, Hugh?

HUGH: That's it exactly. Now, Chris, my boy, the best way to go to the essentials of the problem is to start with unambiguous moral principles. The salary of a member of parliament at this time is a thousand a year. Added to that he has seven hundred and fifty a year towards his expenses untaxed. There's seventeen-fifty right off. Enough to turn marriage into something better than a dream. Then your wife keeps on working for a while as a private secretary, and you continue to preach on Sundays; there's around fifteen-hundred or more towards starting out in life. The sum is correct, Dic?

DIC: Basic mathematics and morals.

HUGH: Now, Dic and I look at this little girl quite simply as the apple of our eyes. You've ventured to become responsible for her happiness. And we want to help you. There'll be incredible competition for my place as parliamentary candidate for the Socialist Party. But we want to make

	arrangements now, some four months before anyone knows about my elevation, so that the succession will be easy and certain for you and Dot. That's the offer, my boy. We're sacrificing a good deal for your sake.
CHRIS:	Mr Hughes, Uncle Dic, I'm surprised. I'm truly grateful, of course, more grateful than I can say . . . But there are difficulties, Mr Hughes.
HUGH:	Yes, yes, true enough. But remember, some of our M.P.s can earn another thousand a year through extra things. You can overcome that sort of difficulty, you'll learn how to manage remarkably soon.
CHRIS:	Yes, thanks. But there are other kinds of difficulties too, Mr Hughes.
HUGH:	Other kinds? Really? Nothing's hard but getting one's bread and cheese.
CHRIS:	You see, I'm not a member of the Labour Party. I've never been a member.
HUGH:	No, no. Shyness. A natural and pleasant quality in a young man. Just like Elijah, my boy. He wasn't one of the prophets until the mantle of Elias fell upon him.
DIC:	You belong to this Nationalist Party, *Plaid Cymru*, they tell me.
CHRIS:	I addressed one of their meetings tonight.
DOT:	But so much has happened since then, Chris.
CHRIS:	I wouldn't like to have the name of . . . a backslider, of having turned my back on them, Dot.
DIC:	Chris, my friend Hugh here was a nationalist until I convinced him. I'm a Welsh-speaking Welshman. But I've never believed, any more than Keir Hardie did, that there's any meaning to the term "nationalism" in Wales.
CHRIS:	You don't believe in Wales?
DIC:	Politically? No . . . My business is politics. I know what's what in politics. I look at India, Ireland, Rhodesia, the Congo, Algeria: I recognize at once that political entity, a nation, a political nation. Nationalism there is a matter of life, a matter of blood. It must be taken very seriously. For at least four centuries no act has occurred in Wales to suggest that there's a political nation there. Political nationalism is only self-deception in Wales. It doesn't exist.

CHRIS: We fight parliamentary elections every year, just like you.

DIC: *(Smiling pleasantly)* Just so. You compete with us on our
            own ground and we control the conditions. That is,
            you're one of the English political parties, exactly like us,
            but you're the party of Don Quixote, just as happy and
            just as successful. Who can take you seriously? My boy,
            leaving a party like that isn't backsliding; it's simply
            growing up.

CHRIS: I need time to think. I can't decide —

DOT: We *have* decided to get married, Chris.

CHRIS: Get married! Yes, of course.

DOT: And this is the only way.

CHRIS: To change my calling? The only way? If I were sure —

DOT: Daddy's sure. Otherwise he won't go into the House of
            Lords. And our getting married depends on that.

HUGH: In the crypt of the House of Commons.

DOT: You hear, Chris? A wedding in the crypt! The crypt of the
            House of Commons.

HUGH: My final appearance in the lower House.

DIC: There's a great deal to be done if you accept the offer.
            We'll have some seven months before an election.
            Perhaps five months before choosing a candidate. We'll
            go about it very quietly. A note in the local papers first, in
            Cardiff, Swansea and Aberystwyth and Caernarvon, that
            the popular young minister, the Reverend Christmas
            Jones, has been accepted as a member of the Labour
            Party. Then Hugh here, who's a deacon and an M.P., can
            arrange a few engagements to preach in the most
            important villages.

HUGH: Yes, that's very important. But remember, Chris, the
            chapels have changed. Nobody in Wales today wants to
            listen to dogma or theology. The thing that goes today is
            ecumenical preaching, without a suggestion of sectarian
            differences, all the emphasis on peace among nations with
            one another and a message of good will. Just like the
            message of the Welsh League of Youth to the children of
            Vietnam and Ulster. That's the preaching that will
            suggest a successor of the right sort to one of the pillars of
            the House of Commons.

DIC: What's important is getting the people to know you. It's an advantage that you're from the district. Then we'll arrange for you to address some of the Labour clubs.

CHRIS: Is there a way I can see the policy of the Labour Party for Wales before then?

HUGH: You see, Dic? Straight to the heart of the problem. But have no fear, Chris *bach*. You leaders of the nationalists and a number of us M.P.s in the Labour Party have long been accustomed to preaching and making a political address and mixing the two together. Have no fear, the Radical tradition of Wales and the old religious revivals are one and the same, and the Labour Party programme is your Nationalist Party's confession of faith. Joining us is coming home. There you are, that's the inspiring text to win an election.

DIC: Unless we get him as the Labour Party candidate, it doesn't make much difference what he says in the election. After that he votes without question in parliament and there's his career safe until his pension. You suggested a wedding in the Crypt?

DOT: Uncle Dic, it's *our* wedding, but it's Daddy's last big show, before he ascends to the upper House. We'll have the time of our lives, Chris.

DIC: Maybe we can bring a bus-load of Party workers and some of the shop-stewards to the crypt. It would be popular. . . *(Maggie enters in outdoor clothes)* The wedding bells will bury every recollection that you were one of these head-in-the-air nationalists.

MAGGIE: Ring wedding-bells for treason, Hooray.

HUGH: *(Upset)* Maggie! What are you doing here? This is a business meeting. In *my* office!

MAGGIE: I know that, Hugh. That's why I came. I felt it might be *my* business.

HUGH: No-no-no! nothing of the kind, poor Maggie. Very much political business. Dic is here by virtue of his office. You've always washed your hands of it, ever since I went into the House of Commons. And it's my seat in the House of Commons that's being dealt with now. A great deal depends on a worthy succession.

61

MAGGIE:	The crypt of the House of Commons and wedding bells? Save us, does Dic Sarc intend to get married? . . . For the sake of the Party?
DIC:	*(After laughing)* I'd take the daughter today, Maggie, since I lost the mother yesterday.
MAGGIE:	You refused to be married in a chapel. You were wise. Who's being married in a crypt today?
DIC:	Not Maggie Evans of the Manse. But her daughter, I hope.
MAGGIE:	The crypt of the House of Commons.
DIC:	That's the plan.
MAGGIE:	You've chosen a member of parliament for her?
DIC:	Here he is.
MAGGIE:	Who?
DIC:	Mr Christmas Jones.
MAGGIE:	Our minister?
DIC:	No less.
MAGGIE:	Willingly?
DIC:	Happily.
MAGGIE:	A member of parliament?
DIC:	To follow Hugh.
MAGGIE:	A change of vocation and a change of party? A one-night revolution!
DIC:	Every conversion is sudden.
MAGGIE:	And to crown it all, Dic Sarc talking the language of Sunday school.
DIC:	The influence of Maggie of the Manse returns.
DOT:	Did you come here to try to prevent our marriage, Mam?
MAGGIE:	I'd give a great deal to return it to what it was before supper. You did fall in love with a minister, didn't you?
DOT:	No. I fell in love with Chris.
MAGGIE:	Bless you, that's the most sensible thing I've heard tonight. But be warned by me, — I have some experience of it, — if Chris of the pulpit is transformed into Chris of the House of Commons, and Chris the nationalist into Chris of the Labour Party, it will be quite difficult for you to recognize your Chris.
DOT:	Your experience is before my time. It's for me and our love —

MAGGIE: That Chris is turning his coat?

DOT: What do you say, Chris?

CHRIS: *(slowly and weightily)* If a man can do this for his love —

MAGGIE: What will he do for his self-respect? Remember the words of another member of the House of Lords: "I could not love thee, Dear, so much, Loved I not honour more."

HUGH: Poor Maggie, you don't understand politics. It's our minister's intention to go to the House of Commons. Well, I have experience too: a man's self-respect goes up and up in the House of Commons.

MAGGIE: And the House of Lords?

HUGH: The pinnacle of the greatness of Great Britain.

MAGGIE: Very well, my lord, show your greatness now. Here's a young man who has preached his way into the heart of your daughter. He confesses that for her sake he's leaving the vocation to which he had a call. He can't afford to marry and remain a minister in London. If he could, he would save his marriage and his self-respect. Give him ten thousand pounds as a wedding present. The blessing of the church and the blessing of the Labour Party will be on your head.

HUGH: *(Cackling wildly as he paces the floor and waves his arms towards her)*
Ten thousand! . . . Ten thousand! . . . Why don't you say ten million? You want to send me to the workhouse before I reach the Lords. That's poisonous of you. Turning a wedding into a chance to bankrupt me. I'd have to sell half my business to raise that amount.

DOT: There's talk of lords losing ten thousand on the Derby.

MAGGIE: I've a pretty fair notion how many ten thousands are in your account. They're not counted on the fingers of only one hand. You have only this daughter to follow you. Your politics isn't the preacher's strong point.

DOT: Mam sees you as a failure, Chris.

DIC: No, no, Dot. She sees ten thousand keeping him a success.

HUGH: You stupid fools! I've given him better than ten thousand already. I've given him a seat in the House of Commons

63

	for life, that will mean ten thousand a year for him before long. A lord's wedding present.
MAGGIE:	Has he accepted it?
DIC:	Does the ten thousand go with his refusal?
DOT:	The girl goes with the seat.
HUGH:	Well, Chris?
	(Dot and Chris look at each other and kiss.)
DIC:	What pulpit can compete?
MAGGIE:	I've tried three times today to save honour. I've been defeated each time by a kiss . . . Goodnight to you all.
DIC:	Where are you going, Maggie?
MAGGIE:	To my sister in Carmarthen.
	(Silent surprise)
DOT:	You'll come to the wedding, Mam?
MAGGIE:	I was at a wedding only once . . . Once too often.
HUGH:	That's my opinion too.
DOT:	That's not Chris's opinion.
DIC:	Chris isn't a member of parliament yet.
CHRIS:	What difference will that make?
MAGGIE:	It will turn a Welsh preacher into an English windbag . . . Good night. *(Exit)*
	(A moment of silence . . . We hear the door shut, then a taxi horn. None of them look at each other. Then suddenly a burst of laughter from Hugh)
HUGH:	Chris, you'll win the election in a walk. That's exactly what she did when I was first chosen as a candidate. I had an easy victory . . . *(Raising his glass)* Excelsior?

THE END

ACADEMIC AFFAIRS

(Problemau Prifysgol, 1962)

While readers and audiences need no assistance to follow the Feydeau-like carryings-on in this fictitious Welsh college, and Sir Gamaliel Price, with his daemonic energy, shameless relish in getting ahead by playing it safe, and pragmatic shrewdness, is an instantly recognizable academic counterpart of *Excelsior's* Hugh Hughes, some information about the University of Wales and one view of its effects on Welsh national identity may be helpful.

The University College of Wales at Aberystwyth was opened in 1872, and two further university colleges were opened at Cardiff in 1883 and Bangor in 1884. All three prepared students for the degrees of the University of London until they were federated as the University of Wales in 1893, which was then authorized to grant its own degrees. Another college of the University was opened at Swansea in 1920; the Cardiff College of Advanced Technology became the University of Wales Institute of Science and Technology in 1967; and St David's College, Lampeter, was united to the University in 1971. At the time *Problemau Prifysgol* (literally "University Problems"; in my titling *Academic Affairs*) was written, the expansion of the University to accommodate a rapidly-growing student population was therefore a plausible basis for Saunders Lewis' invented college of the University of Wales in Powys.

What is not invented is that the University of Wales from its inception was an English-language institution. Such efforts as were made to establish a Welsh-language college as one of its units were unsuccessful during the first century of its existence — a century during which Welsh-language speakers declined from 75% to less than 20% of the population. The case can certainly be made that it has been better for Wales to have had its University on these terms than not at all, but one view of the consequences of this, when combined with the funding of the University as one unit in the complex of British universities, was strongly put by Gwynfor Evans and Ioan Rhys in *Celtic Nationalism* (1968). They stressed the drastic decline in the proportion of Welsh students and staff members after World War II, referring bitterly to "the University of England in Wales", and asserted that

> it is not only students who require enlightenment but national communities. So long as there is no microcosm of Wales at university level, in the Senior Common Room as in the

Students' Union, so long will Welsh thought be the poorer, the Welsh outlook narrower, Welsh problems more intractable, Welsh unity more precarious . . . In the University of Wales, the draught from England . . . has almost blown the Welsh out altogether: in their own university they are condemned to be, not a community, but a clique.

Saunders Lewis had expressed equally strong views concerning the University's contribution to "the crisis of Wales" in his speech on "The Fate of the Language" in 1962, the year in which he created this comedy of other and apparently more immediately urgent "university problems".

CHARACTERS, in the order of their appearance:

Gwen, vice-president of the Student Union
Harri, president of the Welsh Society
Sara Roger, wife of the Professor of Welsh
Sir Gamaliel Price, President of the University College of Wales in
                    Powys
Paul Roger, Professor of Welsh
Ffioretta Davies, Lecturer in Italian
Sam

ACT I

A room that is a kind of private buffet at the back of a dance hall. There is a door to the outside on the right; a door to a cloakroom and a kitchen on the left. There is a table on the left with cups, glasses, jugs. There are a few comfortable chairs here and there. There is a double door in the back to the dance hall; it is open now, and we see young people in their formal evening clothes dancing. Two of them dance into the room – Harri, president of the Welsh Society, and Gwen, vice-president of the Students' Union. They stand. The door closes on the dancers.

HARRI: Better than you expected?
GWEN: The best dance all term.
HARRI: The Welsh Society dance?
GWEN: Strange?
HARRI: Surprising.
GWEN: Why?
     (They move to the table.)
HARRI: Drink?
GWEN: There isn't any.
HARRI: Well, coffee or lemonade?
GWEN: Pop.
HARRI: There isn't any pop. A jug, not a bottle. *(Showing her.)*
GWEN: It's wet?
HARRI: Quite possibly . . . Yes, it's wet.
GWEN: Sopping?
HARRI: Super. *(He pours drinks for them.)*
GWEN: Slop!
HARRI: *Slainte! (They drink.)*
GWEN: Well, why?
HARRI: Why what?

GWEN: Why your surprise that tonight is the best dance all term?

HARRI: The Welsh Soceity?

OWEN: "Call you Ishmael"?

HARRI: Not one of us can do the Twist.

GWEN: I can't do the Twist either.

HARRI: And you're in science!

GWEN: I like science.

HARRI: A Welshwoman?

GWEN: Can't a Welshwoman do science?

HARRI: Not without turning into an Englishman, or an English-woman.

GWEN: Of course. And *you* can't graduate in Welsh without English.

HARRI: You're close to being a nationalist.

GWEN: Schizophrenia is the normal condition of all the Welsh at the University.

HARRI: Except the Welsh Department.

GWEN: The Welsh Department? Sunday school children who have lost their way and found themselves in a betting shop — that's the Welsh Department.

HARRI: Cigarette?

GWEN: *(taking one)* Please.

HARRI: *(after lighting them)* You didn't used to smoke.

GWEN: I started after I had medical assurance that it's a risk.

HARRI: Nonsense! I don't see any value in risk for the sake of risk.

GWEN: I don't see any value in risk *except* for the sake of risk.

HARRI: A little country girl wanting to do wonders!

GWEN: You need salt to give life some savour.

HARRI: But life has savour. Here; tonight.

GWEN: Aren't you fed up?

HARRI: With the college?

GWEN: Well . . . with it being so comfortable for us at our age?

HARRI: How?

GWEN: Grants for everything. Meal-times at the hostel as certain as the sun. Living like a chick in a box. Never the thrill of taking a risk!

HARRI: Are you risking failing the examination?

GWEN: Damn the examination! There's a dance tonight. I never miss a dance.

HARRI: Because a dance is a risk?

GWEN: Oh for a life of experiences and not study!

HARRI: Those of us who study poetry can say that. Experiences are the stuff of poetry.

GWEN: Second-hand experiences, other people's experiences. Science looks towards tomorrow, for new experiences, new answers.

HARRI: In a test-tube.

GWEN: A test-tube can be risky, give you a thrill.

HARRI: There's a difference between experiments and experience. The scientist does experiments, the artist has experiences.

GWEN: You literary people can never see that an experiment *is* an experience.

HARRI: That science is an art?

GWEN: Perhaps. Even in everyday life, looking at people around us, I long to experiment sometimes. Do you?

HARRI: I don't know. How?

GWEN: Put a person in a test-tube. See his reaction. You know?

HARRI: A test-tube?

GWEN: A pickle.

HARRI: Who?

GWEN: *(laughing)* How do I know? Your Professor of Welsh?

HARRI: Roger? Well, I never saw him dance before tonight. I didn't know he could. I thought the *Gogynfeirdd*, the Poets of the Princes, were his only interest.

HARRI: What is your interest?

HARRI: At this moment, you.

GWEN: Getting me into a test-tube? . . . or into a poem?

HARRI: May I kiss you, Gwen?

GWEN: Oh for a life of experiences *and* experiments.
(He kisses her.)

HARRI: That's why I brought you here.

GWEN: That's why I came.

HARRI: You didn't kiss me back.

GWEN: You didn't ask for that.

HARRI: Must I ask?

GWEN: Three times.

HARRI: I'll ask a question first.

GWEN: An examination?

HARRI: A personal question.

GWEN: Risky then.

HARRI: We've known each other for three years, Gwen.

GWEN: "A magic season, a merry summer!"

HARRI: And here we are this year, you the student vice-president and I the president of the Welsh Society.

GWEN: Harri, dear, is this a funeral sermon?

HARRI: I'm afraid of asking my question too quickly.

GWEN: Is there any more of that wet stuff?

HARRI: Lemonade?

GWEN: Thanks.

HARRI: Gwen, the prof says I should be sure of a first in the examination.

GWEN: Roger? He ought to know.

HARRI: Not only that. There's a pretty good chance I'll get the University Fellowship then. Worth six hundred a year.

GWEN: Almost as much as a lecturer's salary.

HARRI: I'm going to work like the devil until I get a chair at the University.

GWEN: Professor Harri Edwards, D. Litt., Wales.

HARRI: D. Litt., Cymru.

GWEN: "*Cymru*" has no university. "Wales, Wales, Pleidiol wyf i Wales." Partial to Wales, that's the University's motto. And that won't continue.

HARRI: Now, Gwen, may we get married right after graduation and go to Ireland for our honeymoon?

GWEN: Ireland?

HARRI: Galway and the isles, the Gaeltacht.

GWEN: To fish?

HARRI: No, for me to master the Gaelic. A splendid way to fill the time.

GWEN: That would be a help — on a honeymoon.

HARRI: Look, Gwen, there's no risk at all. I'm sure of getting a chair. It's a safe venture for you.

GWEN: Are you sure?

HARRI: We can be married the day after the graduation ceremony.

GWEN: Harri, I'm quite fond of you. You have such an original way of proposing. But no, we'd better not get married.

71

HARRI: Of course we'll get married. I won't take no for an answer.

GWEN: You say there's no risk?

HARRI: Like marrying the bank. Three thousand a year before I'm forty. Minimum.

GWEN: I'd be better off dying tonight.

HARRI: You'd be better off dying tonight than refusing me. I'm serious, Gwen.

GWEN: Listen, Harri. If you'd said, Gwen, let's get married tomorrow, next week, before the examination, throw the examination to the dogs, chance losing your first, losing the Fellowship, damn the consequences —

HARRI: Well?

GWEN: I would have agreed.

HARRI: You're mad.

GWEN: For the fun ot it. It would prove that we're young, that we're alive, in love —

HARRI: It would prove that I looked on you as dirt.

GWEN: To me, it would prove that you considered everything dirt but me.

HARRI: Ruining your life and my career?

GWEN: Yes, perhaps. The thrill of taking a risk.

HARRI: That's what love is?

GWEN: Yes, that's what love is. Hasn't it dawned on you?

HARRI: That isn't my idea of love.

GWEN: That isn't your idea of life. Do you know what's the finest thing in the world today?

HARRI: To you? . . . Dancing?

GWEN: Dancing, if you like, but dancing knowing that the Polaris submarines are down there and that some young idiot who's tired, or had a drop too much vodka, can make a mistake —

HARRI: Nonsense, Gwen, nonsense! That doesn't help one to live. Living demands a bit of security —

GWEN: Oh horrors! Security!

(Mrs Roger enters from the left with a plate of sandwiches.)

SARA: Hello! Taking a rest?

HARRI: We came here for a drink, Mrs Roger.

SARA: What did you have?

HARRI: Lemon drink.

SARA: Wasn't it bitter?

GWEN: It was quite safe, Mrs Roger.

SARA: "Safe"? you mean bland?

GWEN: Oh! How did you know?

SARA: That the lemonade is bland?

HARRI: It isn't at all, Mrs Roger. It's fine.

SARA: But safety is bland?

GWEN: Yes, that's it.

SARA: Until you lose it.

GWEN: I see, Mrs Roger. You've been through the war. We haven't. We can never understand each other.

SARA: I'm helping to make sandwiches in the refectory.

HARRI: You shouldn't!

GWEN: Do you need more help, Mrs Roger?

SARA: Miss Davies promised, if called on.

HARRI: From the Italian Department?

GWEN: She's dancing at the moment.

SARA: *(unconcernedly)* With the Professor?

GWEN: With Harri here a while back.

HARRI: No she wasn't!

GWEN *(sotto voce)* Don't be stupid.

HARRI: Oh! yes, of course. Before you absorbed all my attention. I forgot.

GWEN: A number of the staff are dancing. You should be too.

SARA: Have you seen the Principal?

HARRI: Who?

SARA: Sir Gamaliel?

HARRI: He's in an asylum in London.

GWEN: "A private nursing home."

SARA: He's back. He's promised to be here.

HARRI: At the Welsh Society Dance? The Principal?

GWEN: Why not, if he's back?

HARRI: I've never seen the Principal at a dance.

GWEN: Because you never go, except to the Welsh Society's.

HARRI: The all-colleges dance!

GWEN: Yes, you were at that. But in Aberystwyth.

HARRI: Mrs Roger, why is he coming tonight?

SARA: I don't know why I came myself.

HARRI: The wife of the Professor of Welsh! You ought to be our guest of honour.

SARA: I came to help the women, not to be a guest or to dance.

GWEN: Not to look after the Professor, Mrs Roger?

HARRI: The Professor is as sound as a nut, thank goodness.

GWEN: Is he as innocent as his pupils?

HARRI: She's a wicked one, Mrs Roger. You know what she said about the Welsh department?

SARA: The staff or the students?

GWEN: Not the staff, anyway. The staff are all as safe as deacons.

HARRI: Well, we can say this: no other department on the Arts' side publishes as much research work.

SARA: The others don't need to.

HARRI: Why not?

GWEN: Because there are fewer chairs of Welsh and the competition is much fiercer. Right, Mrs Roger?

SARA: Perhaps scholarship has replaced preaching today as the most respectable work in Welsh-speaking Wales.

GWEN: There you are, Harri!

HARRI: Did the Professor graduate before he asked you to marry him, Mrs Roger?

SARA: *(after a moment of laughter)* That's hard to answer . . . He didn't ask.

GWEN: What?

SARA: He put a notice of our engagement in the paper . . . And I didn't object.

HARRI: A Welsh-language paper?

SARA: I suppose.

GWEN: The Bulletin of the Board of Celtic Studies?
(Sir Gamaliel enters from the street. He wears an overcoat over his dinner clothes; he looks successful and distinguished.)

SARA: Sir Gamaliel!

SIR G: My dear Mrs Roger!

SARA: Fully recovered?

SIR G: A pleasant rest. A little break. All's well.

SARA: When did you come back?

SIR G: I arrived last night by train. Work was calling. "When duty whispers."

SARA: This is Miss Gwen Macduff, the student vice-president.

GWEN: Welcome back, sir, and good health.

SARA: Mr Harri Edwards, president of the Welsh Society.

SIR G: I like to see the Welsh-speaking Welsh. A desirable element in the life of the University.

HARRI: You'll have a great welcome in the hall, sir. No one expected such an honour.

SIR G: Thank you, my boy. Yes, the Welsh Society. You must hold onto it, mind. This bi-lingual element gives a bit of special character to the colleges in Wales, so that we are not exactly the same as every "red-brick". I have always held that a bit of colourful variety is the chief need of all the provincial universities. And that is what the Welsh language contributes. You're only a minority, of course, but there is a place for the bi-lingual Welsh. For the time being, at least . . . And the professor? Professor Roger, where is he?

SARA: At the dance, Sir Gamaliel. Will you go in to him? You had better leave your coat. Will you take care of it, Miss Macduff?

GWEN: I'll put it in the cloakroom.

SARA: That would be best.
        (The Principal puts his wallet in the pocket of his coat and gives it to her.)

SIR G: Will it be safe there?

GWEN: I'm leaving my handbag there too. They'll be quite safe.
        (Gwen exits.)

HARRI: May I tell the Professor you're here, sir?

SIR G: No, my boy. I shall stay here to rest for a bit and go in to you later.
        (Harri exits to the dance, and the open door in the back gives a glimpse of Roger and Ffioretta dancing.)

SIR G: Is this room private, Mrs Roger?

SARA: A room for the staff and the officers of the dance. The usual buffet is at the other end of the hall.

SIR G: Very good. I was hoping to see you privately for a few minutes.

SARA: See me?

SIR G: It was for your sake that I came here, Mrs Roger. It was for your sake that I came back to Powys.

SARA: Before you were better, Sir Gamaliel? Did you come back before you finished your treatment?

75

SIR G: No no no, don't worry. The hint did me good.

SARA: Hint? I never gave you any hint.

SIR G: No, it wasn't you, not you at all. But I did receive a hint.

SARA: A hint to return?

SIR G: Because I am needed here. You know, it is strange and surprising, but it's true that it is not entirely a disadvantage for a man in my position to have been raised on a Welsh-speaking hearth.

SARA: Sir Gamaliel! You're talking like a nationalist.

SIR G: Please, Mrs Roger, don't use such foul, filthy words. There's no need for us to be disgusting. After all, we are discussing a university, *universitas.*

SARA: And the Welsh-speaking hearth?

SIR G: A Non-Conformist hearth. Of course I have gone back to the Old Mother, the Established Church, but there is one element in the Welsh Non-Conformist tradition that is important for this college in Powys and indeed for the whole university.

SARA: You're speaking of the Welsh language?

SIR G: You didn't have a university education, Mrs Roger?

SARA: Not at all.

SIR G: I suspected that. It's easily seen.

SARA: You were talking about a Welsh hearth?

SIR G: Yes, because of the respect we Welsh have for a proper appearance, for decency and a good name. Of course the universities in England have moved a long way from the standards of the Victorian age; even Oxford, more's the pity. But, whatever is possible at Oxford, the University of Wales continues to be morally pure. We cannot allow anything improper, anything that borders on — well, on scandal, to be linked with the staff of our colleges in Wales.

SARA: I was in the civil service before I was married, Sir Gamaliel.

SIR G: But Her Majesty's civil service is as respectable as the University of Wales.

SARA: Oh no! The only thing not respectable in the civil service is collecting gossip.

SIR G: May I ask you a somewhat personal question, Mrs Roger?

SARA: Of course. I was a clerk in the Ministry of Pensions. All our questions were personal questions.

SIR G: Mrs Roger, have you received an anonymous letter or letters in the past fortnight?

SARA: Sir Gamaliel! . . . Of course I knew that you were ill. But I never thought that you would do a thing like that.

SIR G: What?

SARA: The two anonymous letters?

SIR G: Yes?

SARA: *You* wrote them?

SIR G: What? . . . Me? . . . You dare to insult me that way! Do you know to whom you are speaking? Do you remember my position? Remember that the Council of the college summoned me all the way from Hong-Kong to be the principal of this technical college and elevate it to one of the colleges of the University of Wales? That there was no one through the whole of Wales who was fit for the position?

SARA: Does that give you a right to send anonymous letters?

SIR G: You demented woman! Do you know that we have a law of slander in Great Britain? That I could take you before a court of law? Silence you forever and ruin you?

SARA: For asking a personal question? Or for speaking the truth?

SIR G: For saying that I, the first-vice-chancellor of the University, send out anonymous letters about the behaviour of a member of the staff.

SARA: So you know what was in the letters?

SIR G: Certainly I know. That is why I came back in such haste.

SARA: Sir Gamaliel, I haven't told a living soul what was in the letters. I haven't told my own husband.

SIR G: You haven't told the professor?

SARA: He's the last person I'd tell.

SIR G: In that case it will be necessary for me to tell him . . . Duty is not always a pleasure.

SARA: Trying to drive me into accusing my husband of being unfaithful to me, was that the purpose of the letters?

SIR G: An interesting question, Mrs Roger. I can't answer it. It would be necessary to know the author of the letters to understand his purpose.

SARA: Then how did you know I was receiving anonymous letters?

SIR G: My dear woman, you said so. I asked you and you answered yes.

SARA: Are you confused, tell me, or am I? Why did you ask? How did you know the contents of the letters?

SIR G: Steady, Mrs Roger, steady. Now you're beginning to get to the nub. Where did your first letter come from? From Bangor?

SARA: Dear heavens! Yes, from Bangor.

SIR G: And the second letter, a letter without a stamp, wasn't it? You had to pay five pence to the postman at the door?

SARA: Yes! Because it didn't have a stamp!

SIR G: From Aberystwyth?

SARA: How do you know?

SIR G: Observe, Mrs Roger, the first was not posted from here, nor the second. Not from London either, and I was in London until yesterday. First Bangor, then Aberystwyth. And by the time he reached Aberystwyth the author of the letters did not have enough cash to pay for two stamps.

SARA: Two stamps?

SIR G: One for your letter and one for the letter to *me*.

SARA: You also received a letter?

SIR G: Two. One from Bangor and the second without a stamp from Aberystwyth.

SARA: Typed?

SIR G: That is easily understood.

SARA: I don't understand anything about it.

SIR G: My dear Doctor Watson! I suspected who could have sent the letters even in London. But I wanted to be certain that you had received two similar letters.

SARA: But Bangor and Aberystwyth?

SIR G: What do you make of that?

SARA: The two most notorious towns for gossip in the whole of Wales.

SIR G: In all fairness, the letters did not come from the divinity schools.

SARA: How do you know?

SIR G   It was one of our students who posted the letters.

SARA: From Bangor and Aberystwyth?

SIR G: Certainly. The all-colleges week. That is why he could not afford a stamp by the time he reached Aberystwyth.

SARA: Sir Gamaliel, I don't see any trace of confusion in your mind.

SIR G: My complaint was not in my mind. That is a weakness that belongs to the staff. But I never go near the staff common room. We principals are a class apart.

SARA: Of course. The County Club. It's no wonder your nerves broke down.

SIR G: When this second letter came, I mended like a boy. Scandal among the members of the staff? Never while I am principal.

SARA: So you accept the testimony of anonymous letters?

SIR G: There's never smoke without fire. And who knows better than the students? Do you know if these accusations are true?

SARA: More than likely. They're too malicious not to be true.

SIR G: What are you going to do, Mrs Roger?

SARA: He is my husband.

SIR G: I was thinking of that.

SARA: I burned the two letters at once. What do you intend to do, Sir Gamaliel?

SIR G: Oh! Fortunately I have my position. I shall protect the university, the good name of the university, the morals of the university. My duty is clear.

SARA: The University is an institution. This college is an institution, a kind of machine —

SIR G: An institution for which I am responsible, for its good name, for keeping it from injury to its reputation —

SARA: Sir Gamaliel, it's better to injure an institution, even the good name of an institution, than to hurt people, than to hurt a person. An institution cannot feel, an institution cannot be embittered for life, an institution doesn't have a wife and children —

SIR G: We who belong to the institution can suffer, all of us. Something like this is exactly the same sort of thing as smallpox, it is contagious. Think of the effect on the students, seeing one of their teachers, especially the professor of Welsh, unfaithful to his wife. Here, at the college! With a woman who is a lecturer! Who was born in Italy! A character in an Opera! It is incredible! a disgrace! Consider the example! Do you know that some of our students get married on their grants? What would the County Councils say?

SARA: I'm married too.

SIR G: You? You? . . . Save us all, so you are! I was forgetting. I was preparing my address to the College Council.

SARA: You can't go to the College Council on the strength of two letters without a name on them.

SIR G: And one of them without a stamp as well . . . Yes, I agree, Mrs Roger, it is necessary to look for more evidence. It is necessary to have proof, proof —
(The door to the hall opens and Paul Roger and Ffioretta Davies come in. She is a beautiful young woman, wearing a daring and artfully simple frock.)

PAUL: Sir Gamaliel! . . . As welcome as an August apple!

SIR G: Good evening Roger . . . How do you do, my dear Miss Davies.

FFIOR: *Che sorpresa, caro rettore!*

PAUL: Fully recovered?

SIR G: "When duty whispers" . . . A person must be capable . . . The Italian Society Dance?

FFIOR: The Welsh Society, *signorone.*

SIR G: Forgive me. I suppose it must be. That is why Mrs Roger is here.

FFIOR: *(kissing Sara warmly) Carissima* Sara!

SIR G: Do you go to the Italian Society dance, Mrs Roger?

PAUL: My wife isn't a member of the staff, Sir Gamaliel.

SIR G: Ah! Some teachers' wives are more on the staff than others.

FFIOR: The Welsh-speaking Welsh on the staff come to the Welsh Society dance to show their side.

SIR G: Yes, there is certainly nothing improper in showing a *side.*

SARA: There's nothing wrong with your frock, Ffioretta.

FFIOR: Did you get my letter, *caro rettore?*

SIR G: From Aberystwyth?

FFIOR: Yes. We had a meeting of the board of examiners there, and I went in the car and posted it there. But you received it safely?

SIR G: Without a stamp on it?

FFIOR: Didn't I put a stamp on it? *Mea culpa, mea culpa, signorone!* I'm truly sorry. I wrote the address at the examiners' meeting. Hastily, you see. I had to run for the post and I forgot the stamp. Oh dear, did you have to pay the extra?

SIR G: Five pence.

FFIOR: And when you were in hospital! Oh, Sir Gamaliel! I don't have my purse at this moment. But you must allow me to pay the five pence.

SIR G: Don't trouble yourself, my dear lady. The knowledge was worth five pence.

FFIOR: The knowledge? That I'm seeking another position? Well, really!

SIR G: And what about Mrs Roger?

FFIOR: Mrs Roger?

SIR G: Will you pay her too?

FFIOR: Pay Mrs Roger?

SIR G: Compensation.

FFIOR: Pay compensation! . . . Oh Paul! He knows everything!

PAUL: Sir Gamaliel, you're interfering in a personal matter —

FFIOR: May I ask you, sir, how you know? Who told you? What right have —

SIR G: *You* did, in your letter —

FFIOR: *I* did?!

PAUL: Ffioretta! . . . Did you?

SARA: This is just like singing a rondo.

SIR G: Mrs Roger, I've said it already. I must in virtue of my position —

FFIOR: By heaven! If I didn't know that you are under a doctor's care —

SIR G: I have been in a private hospital suffering from the shingles. I have been drinking a pint of cream a day and resting. That is the treatment. And you, some of you, were kind enough to hope I would never come back.

PAUL: It's no wonder you're developing a double chin, Sir Gamaliel.

SIR G: But after I received this letter from Aberystwyth, — from Aberystwyth, if you please — I came back straight away.

FFIOR: But why did you need to, Sir Gamaliel, why? All I asked for was a letter of recommendation. You could have sent it through the post.

SIR G: Recommendation? A recommendation from me? here, in the University, The University of Wales? Miss Davies, I can only hope that things have not gone too far. That is the most important part of a principal's work, to preserve the good name of the institution that has been placed in his care, to prevent any scandal —

FFIOR: It was five pence, *caro rettore*, only five pence!

SIR G: It is worth a great deal of sacrifice to smother scandal. I'm sure that Professor Roger, who is such a responsible member of the *senatus* of our college, will confirm that. That is why I came back, Miss Davies, so that we may have a talk about this tomorrow. And now, Mrs Roger, I will go into the hall to see the Welsh Society of the College dancing. *Haec otia studia fovent . . . (And he exits to the hall.)*

FFIOR: *E matto! Matto! Imbecille!*

SARA: There's nothing wrong with his mind.

FFIOR: Sara, I'm trying for a position at the University of London, and I sent to him in London to ask for a letter of recommendation in reference to the job.

SARA: He didn't get your letter.

FFIOR: But you heard him say that I forgot the stamp.

SARA: He was mixed up. It's quite natural. We were talking about a letter he'd received from Aberystwyth when you came in and said that you'd written to him from Aberystwyth.

FFIOR: He had two letters from Aberystwyth?

SARA: No, one. With no name on it.

PAUL: An anonymous letter?

SARA: No name, no stamp.

FFIOR: When?

SARA: The day before yesterday.

FFIOR: I posted my letter the day before yesterday.

SARA: And he left London before yesterday's post.

PAUL: How do you know?

SARA: He said so.

FFIOR: Said what?

SARA: That he'd received an anonymous letter from Aberystwyth. It wasn't your letter.

PAUL: Then what has it to do with Ffioretta?

SARA: Didn't you hear him? He's in better health now than he's been since he left Hong-Kong.

PAUL: But Ffioretta?

SARA: Of course. That's what's cured him.

PAUL: Ffioretta has cured him.

SARA: And you.

PAUL: What are you suggesting?

SARA: That the principal has recovered and is happily preparing a report to the college council.

FFIOR: Paul! I see it all clearly! *Un porco traditor!* An anonymous letter!

PAUL: To the principal?

FFIOR: From Aberystwyth!

SARA: Without a stamp!

FFIOR: *Traditore!* Traitor! Traitor!

PAUL: Sara, did the principal tell you what was *in* the anonymous letter?

SARA: He is very eager to smother scandal.

PAUL: What is the accusation?

SARA: Did you ever receive an anonymous letter, Paul?

PAUL: Never; of course not. Why? Did you?

SARA: I was in the Ministry of Pensions before I was married.

FFIOR: What? Do old-age pensioners write anonymous letters?

SARA: Some of them. Old-age pensioners, widows, mothers, neighbours.

FFIOR: To say what?

SARA: To say whether a neighbour or someone else was earning an occasional ten shillings without declaring it while drawing a pension. Envy is often the reason.

PAUL: And malice. No one ought to put faith in them.

SARA: I learned one thing at the Ministry.

PAUL: That they're all lies.

SARA: No. Most of the time they were true. The best weapon of malice is the truth.

PAUL: Oh! . . . And this letter to the principal? Are you suggesting . . . ?

FFIOR: *Caro amico*, I wonder if it would not be best to tell Sara now? We can't go on like this.

PAUL: No, we can't go on like this.

FFIOR: It had to come to light.

PAUL: What was in the anonymous letter, Sara?

SARA: Don't you know?

FFIOR: Let me talk to Sara. It's easier for me. I'm not related to her like you.

SARA: That is a comfort to us both, Ffioretta.

PAUL: You're welcome to tell her, if she doesn't already know.

SARA: I'll do my best to help you, Ffioretta.

FFIOR: You understand, Sara, Paul and I are at the college every day, we are forced to meet so regularly —

SARA: And you have so many things in common —

FFIOR: Yes, yes, literature, poetry, —

SARA: Music, scholarship —

FFIOR: The students too, *la vita intellettuale* -

SARA: Coffee at eleven every morning in the common room —

FFIOR: Yes, yes, meeting for coffee, conversation, the interest growing —

SARA: Then going for a stroll in the gardens to continue the discussion —

FFIOR: Yes, going for a stroll, sometimes losing ourselves for hours in talk —

SARA: It's dinner time and there's no one else in the gardens, and suddenly —

FFIOR: Yes, Sara, exactly like that, finding ourselves kissing, not thinking —

SARA: And then looking forwards to tomorrow —

FFIOR: Yes, tomorrow and tomorrow! . . . Oh! Sara! How do you know? How do you know?

SARA: How do I know? . . . Jealousy, Ffioretta, jealousy can imagine it, can go through the experience . . . You've fallen in love?

FFIOR: We love each other passionately, Sara. Like Paolo and Francesca, it was a book which bound us in a kiss. Oh I know you can never understand it. Perhaps you can never forgive it. But Sara, I beg you to accept it, to recognize it, to realize that there is no help, nothing else was possible — was it, Paul? — nothing else. Indeed, I want to venture to ask you to help us, because we're in big trouble.

SARA: As much as the principal?

FFIOR: He doesn't know anything about trouble.

SARA: That's why you're looking for a position in London?

FFIOR: She understands, Paul! Bless her, she understands and for-
        gives and is ready to help!
PAUL: Going to London is the only way out.
FFIOR: Paul darling, that's certain. There's no other way.
SARA: Do you believe you can forget Paul in London?
FFIOR: What?
SARA: In London . . . can you forget Paul?
FFIOR: Forget Paul? I can never forget Paul! It's impossible for me
        to live without Paul. I can't imagine living without Paul . . .
        Oh Paul!
        (She presses her hands together and gazes at him.)
PAUL: Ffioretta and I are thinking of you, Sara. Our hearts are
        bleeding for you —
SARA: *(like someone sympathizing at a funeral)* Of course. Nothing
        could be more clear.
PAUL: We've said many times, if this had only happened to anyone
        else but you. That's why we decided that it's necessary for us
        both to go away from here. Leave Wales. Our staying here
        would make life terribly painful for you. I'd do anything to
        spare you pain.
SARA: You're going to London too?
PAUL: That's the plan, to start with anyway.
SARA: There's no chair of Welsh at the University of London.
PAUL: That's true. But it's necessary to sacrifice something.
        There's no love without sacrifice.
FFIOR: Paul, you should have been born in Florence. You are the
        only Welshman who understands love like the people of
        Italy.
SARA: How will you live in London? Keep house for Ffioretta?
PAUL: We've discussed that. There's a hope I will get classes in
        modern literature and drama, night classes —
FFIOR: And finish your work on the *Gogynfeirdd* at the British
        Museum each morning.
PAUL: And then the holidays —
FFIOR: Palermo — Napoli —
PAUL: Pisa at Easter —
FFIOR: Living completely for love and study, art and literature;
        experiences of love and artistic experiences together —
PAUL: You see, Sara. Ffioretta has lived so much in Italy; she was

born there! That's where she was at school! She has opened my eyes to the endless wealth of experiences that are possible when love and scholarship are equally shared by two lovers —

FFIOR: When the inspiration of love awakens the inspiration of scholarship —

PAUL: And the inspiration of scholarship follows the light in the eyes of love.

FFIOR: You understand now, don't you, Sara?

SARA: There's just one thing I cannot understand.

FFIOR: *Carissima!*

PAUL: What can't you understand, Sara?

SARA: Why must you wait until you go to London?

PAUL: I don't follow you.

SARA: Have you gone to bed with Ffioretta? Fucked her?

PAUL: Really, Sara! What a question!

SARA: Coarse? immodest?

PAUL: Well, to put it bluntly, a bit.

SARA: Will you answer me? Have you? . . . I might as well know.

PAUL: Well! . . . not bed yet.

SARA: Between you and me, Ffioretta — bed would be much more convenient.

FFIOR: It would, oh it would. Much more convenient.

SARA: Do you have a bed?

FFIOR: Do you think I am a pig?

SARA: I haven't seen your bed.

PAUL: What is this leading to?

SARA: To Ffioretta's bed. Why must you wait until you go to London?

PAUL: You're willing for me to go to her?

SARA: You've gone already. I can't stop you.

PAUL: Tonight.

SARA: Why not?

FFIOR: Oh Paul!

PAUL: Are you serious, Sara?

SARA: Are you?

PAUL: I had thought of escaping to London first and writing from there to tell you the whole thing.

SARA: Tonight would be better.

FFIOR: It was our prayer as we were dancing just now, Paul.

PAUL: But we didn't dare to hope.

FFIOR: Are you giving him to me, Sara? Surrendering him?

SARA: Not at all. But marriage is not a prison.

PAUL: Really?

FFIOR: Love is freedom, freedom.

SARA: Have you a hot-water bottle?

FFIOR: A hot-water bottle?

SARA: His feet are always cold in bed.

FFIOR: *(laughing triumphantly)* His feet won't be cold tonight, Sara dear.

SARA: *(to Paul)* We'd better go pack.

PAUL: Pack what?

SARA: Pajamas. She says she has a bed. A robe. A clean shirt for tomorrow. And an everyday suit.

PAUL: I can pick those up on the way.

SARA: A toothbrush. Razor; shaving cream. I'm sure she doesn't have shaving cream. I suppose she doesn't.

PAUL: What does that matter tonight?

SARA: You have a nine o'clock lecture tomorrow morning.

PAUL: I'll go pack by myself.

SARA: Paul darling, you haven't packed to go to an overnight committee meeting in Shrewsbury since we were married. You'll be much too nervous tonight; you'd forget everything. Come on, we'll go now. And you can come back here to fetch Ffioretta to her flat.

(Sara exits.)

FFIOR: I'm afraid of losing you, Paul.

PAUL: I'll hurry back. We've won, Ffioretta.

FFIOR: *(kissing him)* Caro! Caro!

(Paul exits. Ffioretta sits down and stretches on a comfortable chair, and then breaks out in long, silent laughter, with her arms above her head. The door on the right opens and Sam stands half in and half out, looking at her for a spell without her knowing he is there. He has the appearance of a tramp, bearded and untidy and poor. The look on Ffioretta makes him smile.)

FFIOR: *(suddenly noticing Sam and leaping to her feet)* Who are you?

87

(Sam comes in and shuts the door. He is young and handsome, he has a light tenor voice and speaks in a cultured way.)

SAM: You know, that's one of the oddest experiences of my life.

FFIOR: What?

SAM: Seeing a woman who's young, but fully, fully mature, all by herself and delighted with herself. Something great has just happened to you.

(Ffioretta, startled, sits down weakly)

FFIOR: Who are you? . . . . Where did you come from?

(He sees the plate of food on the table.)

SAM: May I help myself? *(attacking the sandwiches hungrily)*

FFIOR: You're hiking? In need of food?

SAM: Food; clothing; money; a bath; a drink too . . . Is this something to drink? . . . Lemon drink. Of course. *(drinking)* . . . There's a dance in there? *(pointing to the hall)*

FFIOR: A student dance.

SAM: Staff too?

FFIOR: Some of the staff. The Welsh Society.

SAM: So I heard at the house. Is the gaffer there?

FFIOR: The Professor of Welsh? You were at the house?

SAM: *(cautiously)* I only called there. Called to ask.

FFIOR: Do you know him?

SAM: What's his name?

FFIOR: Paul — Paul Roger. He'll come back shortly.

SAM: Here? . . . And you're waiting for him . . . That's why you were laughing?

FFIOR: *(becoming angry)* Signore!

SAM: Oho! . . . *Signore!* . . . Then you're a lecturer, aren't you? A lecturer in Italian? . . . Of course . . . That frock is from Florence. One of the posh little shops near the Ponte Vecchio, right? Smashing!

FFIOR: *(sitting very straight and trying to be severe)* Young man!

(Sam suddenly looks past her and points to the door behind her.)

SAM: Here's Paul!

FFIOR: *(turning and leaping to her feet)* Paul!

SAM: *(collapsing in laughter)* Well, well, well! upon my life! . . . Has this Paul asked you to marry him?

FFIOR: *(on her feet trembling with anger)* Get out of here at once, at once!

(Sam casually takes another sandwich.)

SAM: On second thoughts, no; he hasn't proposed marriage. A woman doesn't laugh all by herself like that on that occasion. It was the laughter of conquest I saw from that door, not the laughter of love. You've caught him; right? You're waiting for him here; he can't escape; you've got him where you wanted him; he's in your hand.

FFIOR: *(excitedly)* I'll call for the police if you don't get out of here at once.

SAM: You won't, pretty lady. You must wait for him here. It's important. Like waiting for Godot.

FFIOR: Why are you here? What is your business?

SAM: A job. I have some work to do here.

FFIOR: You know that this is the University College?

SAM: That's why I came.

FFIOR: A new lecturer?

SAM: Hardly. Look at me.

FFIOR: I'm forced to. What is your work?

SAM: Blackmail. I wonder what the Welsh word for that is. A professional black-mailer, that's me!

FFIOR: *(weakly)* What hold do you have on . . . ?

SAM: *(delighted)* On Paul? Paul Roger? None at all, my dear girl, none at all. I've never hear his name before. I didn't know he existed. Paul Roger is in your hands, not mine.

FFIOR: *(sinking into a chair)* Thank goodness! *Dio mio,* I had a fright.

SAM: You gave me the chance. I caught you without a mask on your face. An opportunity to get a little practice, you know; essential for a performing artist.

FFIOR: You're disgusting.

SAM: That's me, to a T. You and I have a lot in common. Of course, you're only a beginner?

FFIOR: Who are you? What's your name?

SAM: Sam. Call me Sam.

FFIOR: Sam what?

SAM: It varies. But Sam is a constant. And you?

FFIOR: Miss Davies.

SAM: Haven't you been christened?

FFIOR: *(frowning, then smiling)* Oh, all right! Ffioretta.

SAM: Ffioretta! From Florence, just like the frock. May we be partners, Ffioretta?

FFIOR: You're attacking me like a barrage, without mercy.

SAM: And you have no defences. How old are you?

FFIOR: Sam!

SAM: That's better. Much better. How old are you?

FFIOR: Twenty-seven.

SAM: And Paul?

FFIOR: He's thirty-eight.

SAM: He's married? . . . And a father?

FFIOR: Of course.

SAM: Well, you're a fool, Ffioretta, a silly stupid little woman. You're charming, you're ripe for love, your frock is from Florence, but you're silly and stupid. You can't shape him; he's too long married.

FFIOR: *(searching)* Where is my bag?

SAM: *(without moving)* On the chair.

FFIOR: *(getting it and taking out her handkerchief)* Get out of here. You're insufferable, insufferable.

SAM: *(without moving) La cortesia, signorina!* Say "please, Sam".

FFIOR: Will you —

SAM: Will you please —

FFIOR: Leave me alone.

SAM: *(going suddenly to her and holding her arms)* Say: "will you please leave me alone, Sam".

FFIOR: *(sulky but obedient)* Will you please leave me alone, Sam?

SAM: *(releasing her casually)* All right. For the time being. One lesson at a time, but make sure you remember it.

FFIOR: *(drying her tears)* You're cruel and horrid. You've spoiled my evening.

SAM: Don't worry. Paul will come shortly. So you can play lovers. *(Gwen enters from the hall and stands there.)*

GWEN: Miss Davies! I'm sorry.

FFIOR: That's all right, Miss Macduff. May I introduce you to each other? . . . Miss Gwen Macduff, the student vice-president . . . Mr Samuel Price.

(*Gwen stares at him. And he, with his eyebrows raised in surprise, stares at Ffioretta.*)

SAM: Blackmail!

GWEN: (*with a very gracious bow of her head*) Good evening, Mr Price.

SAM: Good evening, Miss Macduff.

GWEN: (*who is doting on him*) Which university?

SAM: (*smiling*) I'm experiencing shock upon shock. How do you know I was at university?

GWEN: The style.

SAM: Hong-Kong first. Then Melbourne.

GWEN: I knew it. The supper is just over and the band is about to start again. Will you come dance the first dance with me?

SAM: (*in a tone of protest*) Miss Macduff.

GWEN: Gwen, to you. And you — Sam?

SAM: Sam, certainly. Does everyone here at the college work as swiftly as you?

GWEN: (*obvious contempt*) At this college? They're as swift as a gravestone.
(*The three laugh.*)

SAM: I can't go dancing like this.

GWEN: Why not?

SAM: Look at me.

GWEN: That's what I'm doing. I'm staring. A beatnik. The first beatnik ever to venture into a posh dance at the college. Everybody here is so respectably "respectable". Everyone in posh clothes. It will be heavenly to lead you onto the floor. Can you do the Twist?

SAM: I suppose so. And you?

GWEN: Lord, no. Where did you learn?

SAM: Wandsworth. Wandsworth is full of twisters.

GWEN: London, right? One of the University colleges?

SAM: Not a college for women . . . I'd better wash my hands before I lay a hand on that frock.

FFIOR: There's a place to wash in the cloakroom, through that door on your left.
(*Sam exits through the door on the left, and Harri and Sir Gamaliel enter simultaneously from the dance hall.*)

SIR G: Splendid, my boy. Marvellous. I didn't know the Welsh Society was so lively. I was happy to hear the dancers speaking quite as much English as Welsh. A pleasant mixture. It has been my policy to make sure that enough young people come to us from England, students and staff, to keep the college from becoming parochial. I give you credit, the accents of Leeds and Wigan are quite at home here, and that is clearly a healthy influence on the Welsh Society . . . Ah, Miss Davies, *without* the Professor. And where are Professor and Mrs Roger?

FFIOR: Professor and Mrs Roger, *caro rettore*, have gone home.

SIR G: Together?

FFIOR: They started out together. Do you think that's improper?

SIR G: That's pleasant news, Miss Davies. You've been very sensible. And I congratulate you. Yes, of course, this is Miss . . .

OWEN: Gwen Macduff, sir.

SIR G: Right. A pleasant dance, Miss Macduff. Excellent arrangements . . . *(The door on the left begins to open, but Ffioretta puts her hand on the knob and prevents the door from opening. Only Sam's leg and foot are seen.)* . . . And now I would like to get my overcoat.

FFIOR: *(going into the cloakroom)* Right away, Sir Gamaliel. *(Her voice is heard behind the door, quite authoritatively)* No, no, no, not just yet, not tonight.

SIR G: The maids are working in there, Miss Macduff?

GWEN: We girls and some of the staff wives are the maids, sir. *(Ffioretta returns with the overcoat. Sir Gamaliel puts the wallet in the pocket of his suit and makes a bow to the company.)*

SIR G: Good night, my friends. It's nice to see that everything is turning out all right. Without scandal. *(Sir Gamaliel exits. The door to the hall opens. Music in the distance.)*

HARRI: The first dance after supper. May I have it, Gwen?

GWEN: I'm sorry, Harri. I've already promised.

HARRI: To whom did you promise? Gwen, this isn't fair.

GWEN: To Sam the beatnik. Here he is now. *(Sam comes straight to Ffioretta.)*

SAM: Why the devil couldn't I come in with you?

FFIOR: The gaffer. He was here.

(A burst of laughter from Sam)

SAM: You're extremely shrewd, my love . . . Well, Gwen, how about it?

(Gwen can only worship silently. They dance out to the hall.)

HARRI: Who is he, Miss Davies, do you know?

FFIOR: He's here on a visit. From the University of Hong-Kong.

HARRI: It's disgusting swank to dress like that. *(He turns and goes into the hall.)*

(Paul enters with a small suitcase. Ffioretta runs to him.)

FFIOR: Paul! Paul! Come in! Oh I was so afraid . . . *(Paul takes off his overcoat)* . . . I was afraid you wouldn't come back.

PAUL: Everything's fine.

FFIOR: It's fine now. But I had a terrible fright, a nightmare!

PAUL: Music and dance! My darling!

FFIOR: This is the dance of the new life. *La Vita Nuova!*

PAUL: We'll dance all the way to bed.

(They dance out into the hall and the light.)

CURTAIN

ACT II

*The parlour of the Rogers' house. It is in unpretentious good taste –
the taste is Sara's – and comfortable. The telephone rings three or four
times before Sara enters through the door on the left. There are French
windows at the back opening onto the garden – before she picks up the
phone, Sara opens the glass doors on a fine morning. The path to the
front door passes this open glass door. There is a cheque-book on the
table beside the telephone.*

SARA: Powys five-eight — — Yes, it's me, Sara. . . Ffioretta! Well!
. . . Good heavens, what is it, Ffioretta? You're crying! *(She
smiles happily)* . . . Don't cry into the telephone, I can't hear
you. . . Paul's gone! . . . But of course, he's at the college, he
has a nine o'clock lecture . . . You needn't break your heart;
you'll see him at the coffee table at eleven and then go for a
stroll in the gardens: aren't old customs sweet? . . . What?
. . . Stop crying. Ffioretta, the phone is becoming quite
damp . . . You had a fight? . . . Never mind, everyone fights
after the first night. Of course it's different when you're not
married; you're on loan to him, rent-free . . . May you come
here? What for? What do you need to know? . . . A Welsh
breakfast? . . . It's quite simple, porridge — *uwd* — to begin
with, then bacon and two eggs, then toast and marmalade,
and tea of course. He always has China tea for breakfast
before a nine o'clock lecture . . . What? Who? Paul? He went
out without breakfast? Without anything at all? Oh
Ffioretta! What will become of the students? . . . A nine
o'clock lecture without a bit of breakfast after a night of the
old Welsh custom of bundling! That poor honours class! . . .

94

Well, come here if you wish. *Uwd*, porridge? Yes, I'll show you how to make *uwd*. After all, he has to be kept alive — for the sake of the *Gogynfeirdd* . . . Don't you have a lecture this morning? Well, you're welcome to come. Do you have an apron? . . . No, not a napkin. Good heavens — an apron! . . . *(Sir Gamaliel Price, wearing his college gown, approaches the window and she waves her hand at him. He stands there.)*
. . . It's all right, we'll make porridge together. Be here within ten minutes. An apron, remember, not a college gown!
(She puts down the phone and goes to the window.)
. . . Sir Gamaliel! An unexpected visit. Come in.

SIR G: Forgive me for calling so early, Mrs Roger. Is the professor here?

SARA: He's at the college. A nine o'clock lecture. An honours class.

SIR G: A nine o'clock lecture! When he's a professor. Strange, very strange.

SARA: Not in the University Welsh departments.

SIR G: Are they different from the other departments?

SARA: The Welsh Non-Conformist tradition.

SIR G: Of course, of course. I've noticed that too. The lecturers in Welsh have inherited the frown and the cough of the old-time preachers. And the same place in the life of the nation. The same public respectability, except for a few black sheep.

SARA: The tradition of the association and the assembly.

SIR G: "Going to glory" as they lecture, right?

SARA: Three lectures as morning service. Three others as afternoon service. Five days a week.

SIR G: There's jubilation? . . . Staying after?

SARA: Everyone stays after. Before they've come to, the next lecture has begun.

SIR G: He won't come here until eleven?

SARA: He may come earlier today . . . he didn't have any breakfast.

SIR G: Really? . . . Fasting? . . . I hope he isn't leaning towards the papists.

SARA: He has a great interest in Italy.

SIR G: That always goes with a bit of laxness in morals. But in all fairness he went home early from the dance last night.

SARA:	You can see him at the college.
SIR G:	I would rather see him here.
SARA:	Why here?
SIR G:	Privately.
SARA:	Some new trouble?
SIR G:	Sad and disturbing.
SARA:	Another anonymous letter?
SIR G:	Worse.
SARA:	What could be worse? A scandal?
SIR G:	In the Welsh department again.
SARA:	You don't say!
SIR G:	I'm afraid this is a matter that will require calling the police to deal with it.
SARA:	And you want the police to come here to my house rather than to the college for the good name of the University?
SIR G:	For the good name of the department of Welsh, Mrs Roger.
SARA:	This is my home, not the home of the department of Welsh.
SIR G:	The home of the Professor of Welsh.
SARA:	I'm glad to hear it.
SIR G:	Did you doubt it?
SARA:	Perhaps, a bit.
SIR G:	But he came home properly with you last night.
SARA:	Why is there any need for the police?
SIR G:	I would rather discuss that privately with the Professor.
SARA:	Where a man sleeps is not a matter for the police.
SIR G:	Of course not. As long as he doesn't sleep on the highway.
SARA:	No, she has a flat. Besides, I'm the one who arranged it all.
SIR G:	What? You know? . . . Why didn't you say?
SARA:	*I* am his wife.
SIR G:	And you arranged it all? When?
SARA:	Last night.
SIR G:	While I was at the dance?
SARA:	I suppose so. What difference does that make?
SIR G:	And I left the coat and the wallet in your care . . . *(walking in pain and staring at her)* I can't understand you. I can't believe you. Last night at the dance?
SARA:	After you rehearsed your address to the College Council. You remember? An eloquent speech about the purity of the University — nothing indecent is to enter it, and the

smallest possible scrap of Welsh. Well, if you intended to throw my husband out of his job, I had to face the situation; a matter of bread and cheese.

SIR G: *(A short incredulous laugh)* Mrs Roger, you've lost your head. Obtaining bread and cheese — like that!

SARA: Didn't you say that my husband was likely to lose the chair?

SIR G: Things have changed. He went home with you last night, early, in front of everyone. That was as good as showing that this bit of adultery or threat of adultery was over, that everything had returned to regularity and order.

SARA: There's some hope of that, I agree. I've had a hint of fair weather this morning.

SIR G: Then why . . . ?

SARA: Why what?

SIR G: I can't follow you at all.

SARA: Sexual problems, Sir Gamaliel, a married woman's problems. They're not often part of a university's problems. About once every ten years in Wales.

SIR G: Has this happened before?

SARA: Sir Gamaliel!

SIR G: Mrs Roger, consider that the worst happens and he loses the Chair of Welsh and leaves here, goes to London, for example —

SARA: Yes, that was the plan.

SIR G: Well, even in London, he, or you, can't live by stealing. Not at his age! A Professor of Welsh at the University College turning common thief and picking pockets! That isn't his craft. He hasn't had an apprenticeship. A matter of bread and cheese indeed!

SARA: Stealing? . . . Are you feeling quite well, Sir Gamaliel?

SIR G: As well as possible in the circumstances.

SARA What circumstances, sir?

SIR G: One of the college teachers, Mrs Roger, turning to picking pockets! It is something of a novelty. Even in the Department of Welsh!

SARA: Sir Gamaliel, is your mind quite clear?

SIR G: Mrs Roger, I know that you are in a pretty dreadful situation. That is clear. But it would be wise for us to keep this conversation as courteous as we can.

SARA:	It's courtesy to accuse my husband of turning common thief and picking pockets?
SIR G:	Before I came here this morning I didn't dream for a moment that it was possible. It has been a surprise to me.
SARA:	It's been a surprise to me too. Weren't you talking of calling the police here?
SIR G:	Yes, certainly. But that was before I knew.
SARA:	Before you knew what?
SIR G:	That you arranged it all.
SARA:	Who is the thief then, me or Ffioretta or Paul?
SIR G:	The poor College!
SARA:	I remember: according to the Ten Commandments committing adultery is a kind of theft. But I scarcely think that is the view of the police or the law of England.
SIR G:	I am not talking now about the immorality of the staff. That is another problem. This is a worse scandal.
SARA:	Thank you for your courtesy. What *are* you talking about?
SIR G:	I am talking about stealing, taking money, taking twenty pounds and a whole book of bank cheques. Theft . . . You understand, Mrs Roger, that sort of thing is theft.
SARA:	Taking twenty pounds?
SIR G:	Four five-pound notes and a cheque-book.
SARA:	Taking twenty pounds from where? When?
SIR G:	Last night at the dance. The Welsh Society dance. Out of the wallet I put in my coat and left in your care when I went in to the dance.
SARA:	Paul? Are you saying that Paul . . . ?
SIR G:	You're the one who said it, not I. You are the one who confessed. You're the one who arranged it all, you said.
SARA:	And you presume that that is why Paul went home early from the dance? That he picked your pocket and took twenty pounds from the wallet and cleared out? And you came here to demand it before you called for the police? For fear of causing scandal at the college?
SIR G:	Mrs Roger — once again — you were the one, not I —
SARA:	Gamaliel Price, you're going clean off your head! Do you know there is such a thing as the law of scandal? Do you know I could take you to a court of law? Do you know I could chuck every stick of this furniture at your head —

(Sir Gamaliel retreats step by step before her towards the window and falls into the arms of Ffioretta who comes in at that moment.)

FFIOR: *Che sorpresa, caro rettore.*

SIR G: Miss Davies, forgive me. I'm sorry. An unfortunate situation!

FFIOR: *Niente!* I have never had a principal in my arms before.
(She fixes his cravat and his gown which have become untidy.)

SARA: Hold onto him, Ffioretta!

SIR G: But I asked you to meet me in my office at the college, Miss Davies. Not here.

FFIOR: What difference does it make, *caro?*

SIR G: Who told you I was here? My secretary?

FFIOR: *(taking his arm and leading him to a chair)* Never mind who. We can talk just as well here, can't we, Sara? I'm in trouble, Sir Gamaliel, terrible trouble, and you're just the one to help me; Sara knows —

SIR G: In trouble. Miss Davies? Already? A woman on the staff? And I thought the whole thing could be kept private! Don't you take the pill?

FFIOR: No, it isn't that, *caro.* It's a question of losing, not taking.

SIR G: Losing? You too? How much? Twenty pounds?

FFIOR: Much more than twenty pounds.

SIR G: Dear heavens! A cheque!

FFIOR: My life! Everything!

SIR G: It's best to send for the police at once.

FFIOR: No no no *niente!* You're the one who can help me. You're a married man.

SIR G: A widower.

FFIOR: That's even better. Look, Sir Gamaliel, did you have break-fast this morning?

SIR G: Did I have breakfast? Of course I had breakfast. I have an excellent married woman who keeps house for me, and her husband as a servant and my chauffeur. That has nothing to do with —

FFIOR: Yes yes yes. That's the heart of the problem.

SIR G: The problem?

FFIOR: Now then, what did you have for breakfast? Can you remember? Do you know what goes into your mouth?

SIR G: Miss Davies, I have some painful and important things to discuss —

FFIOR: You haven't anything as important as this, Sir Gamaliel. Tell me what you had for breakfast!

SIR G: What I have is a matter of theft, Miss Davies, common theft, not of murder or poisoning. My housekeeper is completely guiltless.

FFIOR: *(passionately) La prima colazione*! Tell me on your oath, Sir Gamaliel, what did you have for breakfast?

SIR G: Mrs Roger, is everyone out of his mind this morning?

SARA: That's a question that interests me too.

FFIOR: I'm not asking an empty question, *caro*. My whole life depends on the answer. Breakfast, breakfast, what did you have —

SIR G: *(with professional patience)* I had breakfast, Miss Davies. A totally normal breakfast. The usual Welsh breakfast.

SARA: The same as everybody else in Wales.

FFIOR: I could scream! The usual Welsh breakfast! Does every living person in Wales eat the same thing between getting out of bed and going out in the morning?

SARA: They probably do.

FFIOR: What did you have, Sir Gamaliel? To eat? What first?

SIR G: First? First, I had porridge, *uwd*.

FFIOR: *(with a loud scream) U-w-d! U-w-d!* The word is exactly like the sound of a person throwing up: *u-w-d!* It's no wonder the Welsh haven't a clue about making love! Who could possibly make love, make love while plates of *u-w-d* like a dog's vomit are constantly passing through his guts!

SARA: *(seriously concerned)* Oh Ffioretta, didn't he have any breakfast at all?

FFIOR: He didn't want anything, not a thing. I had instant coffee; no, he didn't take coffee before eleven. I had a tomato and cream-cracker biscuits; he wouldn't look at them. I had *gelato*, what is that called? *pezzo duro*, in the freezer, — ice cream!

SARA: Ice-cream for breakfast! Ffioretta! On an empty stomach! In this weather! Before a nine o'clock lecture!

SIR G: I can't follow you, Miss Davies. Are you talking about the thief last night? He broke into your flat later?

FFIOR: *(to Sara)* If a person wants food in the morning, Sara! For the academic life, *la vita intellettuale*, ice-cream is light, spiritual, poetic, full of inspiration. You know, if anyone asked for *"uwd"* in any respectable house in Florence, he would be thrown out for making an improper noise. But I know of some of the most brilliant philosophers in Bologna, they live on ice-cream.

SIR G: It isn't philosophers in Bologna that are in question, Miss Davies, but a thief, a common thief. He broke into your flat? Have you notified the police?

FFIOR: Thief? What thief?

SIR G: The thief who took twenty pounds and a complete book of cheques out of the wallet in my overcoat last night during the dance.

FFIOR: Really? Well! . . . He did that? . . . He's a cool one!

SIR G: Cool? You're talking very irresponsibly. I can't judge the matter so lightly. To think there is a person at the college who takes twenty pounds and cheques at a dance and then breaks into the flat of a female lecturer long after midnight! And on top of it all, you offer him ice-cream for breakfast!

FFIOR: But I had nothing else to offer him.

SIR G: Miss Davies, what did you do with him *before* offering him ice-cream?

FFIOR: Paul? You're talking about Paul? Paul didn't break into my flat.

SIR G: He didn't? Thank goodness! The College Council has enough worry with him already . . . Forgive me, Mrs Roger, there must be some misunderstanding . . . Then who broke into your flat, Miss Davies?

FFIOR: *Caro rettore*, no one broke in. Everything was all right, or fairly all right, until this morning.

SIR G: Was it really! He must have been hiding there all night without your knowledge?

FFIOR: Not likely! That's not what he came for!

SIR G: *(standing)* Who are you talking about, Miss Davies?

FFIOR: About Paul of course. There's no one else.

SIR G: Is there more than one Paul?

SARA: Dear Lord, yes. He is legion.

SIR G: Your husband, Mrs Roger? Is he the one who left without the ice-cream?

SARA: Yes, Ffioretta? My husband?

FFIOR: *(sadly)* Yes, yes, worse luck.

SIR G: He slept with you last night? That's what you're saying?

FFIOR: Part of the time. I suppose.

SIR G: *(turning pale with emotion)* Mrs Roger. After the Welsh Society dance! Did you hear! Did you know about this?

SARA: I'm the one who arranged it all.

SIR G: *(collapsing limply into his chair)* May I have . . . a glass of water?

SARA: *(moving to the table by the wall)* Will brandy do the trick?

SIR G: I wouldn't be surprised . . . I need something.

SARA: *(giving him brandy)* I haven't any ice-cream.

FFIOR: You're a devil, Sara, *diavola, diavola!*
(Sir Gamaliel sips brandy, Sara smiles quietly, and Paul comes in through the window and stands there.)

PAUL: Sir Gamaliel Price! I'm sorry not to have been here!

SIR G: *(weakly)* Professor Roger, it is a sorry thing at best that you ever *left* here!

PAUL: The truth and nothing but the truth. But how do you know? Have you had a similar experience? In Hong-Kong?

SIR G: *(still weak from the shock)* Professor Roger —

PAUL: These Welsh colleges go to the ends of the earth to look for principals. That's your advantage. God only knows what some prodigal Welshman has left behind him in Hong-Kong. What if someone from Hong-Kong should return to Wales? He'd have quite a story, Sir Gamaliel!

SIR G: Professor Roger —

PAUL: No, the fault isn't yours, Sir Gamaliel. The council of every college in Wales is sure that Hong-Kong is a palace of learning and valour compared to Bala or Swansea. It takes a massacre or a calamity to cause anyone to look for a principal in Wales.

SIR G: Professor Roger —

PAUL: Why the brandy, Sir Gamaliel? Did you lecture this morning?

SIR G: Lecturing is not part of a principal's job —

PAUL: But you had breakfast, Sir Gamaliel? You had breakfast, didn't you?

SIR G: Professor Roger, it wasn't breakfast but adultery and theft —

PAUL: Instead of breakfast? Adultery and theft? No, not in Wales. In Hong-Kong, I don't know. In Florence and Milan, more than likely. But not in Wales. No, seriously now, Sir Gamaliel, did you have breakfast?

SIR G: Of course I had breakfast.

PAUL: "Of course". Thank goodness for those words! Proof that the cosmos is tidy and rational. I was beginning to have my doubts. What did you have for breakfast, Price?

SIR G: May I have a drop more of that brandy, Mrs Roger? *(She pours brandy for him.)*

PAUL: Did you have porridge, Price? *Uwd?*

SIR G: Of course I had *uwd*.

PAUL: Again "of course"! It's as orthodox as the Ten Commandments. You know I was lecturing on an empty stomach just now to the honours class on the *awdlau'r gorhoffedd*, the poems of praise. "Praise!" And as I was explaining the meaning of the word I could hear the oats of Pentrefoelas sputtering as they boiled on the fire. *U-w-d!* There's music for you, in that word. Deep tender bass music, like the cello of Pablo Casals on the lowest notes in an immortal air of Bach. *U-w-d!*

FFIOR: Sara, *cara*, may I also have a drop of that brandy? *(Sara pours brandy for her.)*

PAUL: Do you know, Sir Gamaliel, I don't know what on earth brought you to this house so early in the morning, but I thank you from the bottom of my heart —

SIR G: *(trying to rise with dignity)* Professor Roger —

PAUL: *(pressing him back into his chair)* No, no, don't apologize. You're welcome here. You've done me a favour. Between you and me, it wasn't so easy for me to come home at an unexpected hour today. It might have been wisest to toss my hat in first the way they once did in Cwm Rhondda and wait to see if it were tossed back or not. But here you are, making everything easy. When I've gone without breakfast, and my stomach is empty, and my head's spinning, after a night of dancing and climbing the rocks of the Harz mountains —

FFIOR: *Becero! Porco! . . . Uwd!*

(She tosses the remains of the brandy from her glass into his face . . . Harri and Gwen come through the garden to the window as Paul is drying his face with his handkerchief.)

SARA: Mr Harri Edwards! Miss Gwen Macduff! Come in.

HARRI: We wanted to see the professor, Mrs Roger.

SARA: He's here. And the Principal. And Miss Davies.

GWEN: Goodness! The Staff Common Room!

SARA: Oh no! The Principal is here.

HARRI: Terrifying!

SARA: We're all terrified.

HARRI: I tried to see you after the nine o'clock lecture, sir.

PAUL: I had to leave earlier than usual.

HARRI: You were briefer than usual too. You didn't look too well, sir.

PAUL: Marking papers, you know . . . And the dance last night.

HARRI: Yes, the dance last night. There's something a bit alarming.

PAUL: Alarming? Connected with the dance? A financial loss?

HARRI: An alarming loss.

SIR G: Alarming, you said?

HARRI: Gwen and I thought we might see the Professor of Welsh privately, sir. It's a matter for the Welsh Society.

SIR G: The dance was open to the College.

GWEN: Much too open.

SIR G: Too open? Then it's a matter for me, the Principal?

HARRI: Perhaps it's a matter for the police, sir.

(Everybody's eyes are on him, startled.)

SIR G: Have you seen the police?

HARRI: I had a nine o'clock lecture. Then I looked for the Professor.

SIR G: Theft?

GWEN: Yes, theft. You know? That's why you're all here?

SIR G: Miss Macbeth —

GWEN: Macduff, sir.

SIR G: Macduff, right. I knew you were somewhere in the play. Why didn't you go for the police? Did you also have a lecture?

GWEN: I am the student vice-president, sir.

SIR G: Forgive me. Of course, you never go to lectures. Then why haven't you seen the police?

GWEN: But the scandal to the College, sir!

SIR G: My dear girl! Such *esprit de corps!* No wonder you were elected vice-president! Roger, this girl would make a wife for a principal!

HARRI: That's what I've said too, sir. You see, Gwen?

PAUL: Where was the theft?

HARRI: In the cloakroom last night, during the dance or at supper time. Someone went through the coats.

GWEN: And the bags.

SIR G: Yes, yes, I know.

HARRI: You sir?

SIR G: My coat was there.

GWEN: I put it there. And my handbag too.

PAUL: I saw them together before I went home.

SIR G: You saw them, Professor Roger?

SARA: I was the one who arranged it.
(The Principal eyes her.)

FFIOR: You've been busy, Sara.

SIR G: I lost twenty pounds and a book of cheques from the wallet in my coat.

GWEN: And I lost four pounds from the handbag.

SIR G: What have you to say, Professor Roger?

PAUL: I'm really afraid that it's a matter for the police.

GWEN: It would do tremendous harm to the college dances.

HARRI: And to the Welsh Society. I can hear the English at the college, "Taffy was a Welshman."

GWEN: But that would be fun, Harri. Just like Sam the beatnik.

HARRI: Is there any way to stop it from going into the hands of the police, sir?

SIR G: Well, if the thief is known, and to spare the good name of the college . . .

SARA: If he were to confess? That's what you mean? You know, I wouldn't be greatly surprised if there isn't a chance.

HARRI: It's someone from the college then? One of the students?

FFIOR: If it were one of the students, that would be a matter of discipline for the College senate.

SIR G: Certainly, student discipline is in the hands of the senate.

I'm afraid that this is a matter for the College Council. Staff discipline.

SARA: Which is your bank, Sir Gamaliel? The "North and South Wales"?

SIR G: Yes. My father's bank, my grandfather's bank, and my bank.

SARA: And the book of cheques you lost, it was a new book?

SIR G: A complete book of sixty cheques — not a one had been used. But how do *you* know that, Mrs Roger? It was in the wallet in my overcoat together with the four five-pound notes.

FFIOR: And they disappeared last night?

SIR G: Is it possible that *you* know where they are, Miss Davies?

FFIOR: *(with a bit of laughter)* No indeed. But I'm beginning to half suspect.

SIR G: Yes, unhappily, that is easy to understand. And you also, Professor Roger?

PAUL: Really, Sir Gamaliel —

SIR G: Wait a minute . . . *(looking at the students)* We're in mixed company here. But may I warn you in my position of principal that you need not say anything at this moment that could distress any member of the College staff — especially you yourself.

SARA: Dear Sir Gamaliel, there's more trouble waiting for us all than you know.

SIR G: Surely *you* have not called for the police, Mrs Roger?

SARA: The police and I aren't such good friends. After all, I am a Welshwoman. But there's a telephone here if you wish to call.

SIR G: I must notify the bank. So the police must be told.

FFIOR: Tell the bank?

SIR G: To stop the cheques.

FFIOR: Of course! Is the thief's writing like yours?

SIR G: How do I know? Didn't you say that he'd spent the night in your flat?

FFIOR: *(intensely)* If only he hadn't . . . *(a contemptuous look towards Paul) Uwd.*

SIR G: So *you* haven't any idea where my cheque book is.

FFIOR: I dare swear it isn't far away.

SARA: No. I agree.

SIR G: *(rising)* Very well, I will call the police before the thief has a chance to escape.

FFIOR: Don't, Sir Gamaliel, I beg you, don't. For the sake of the college, for your own sake. You'll cause trouble.

SARA: Besides, there's no need.

SIR G: No need? Why is there no need?

SARA: Your cheques are quite safe.

SIR G: How can they be safe?

SIR G: I have your cheque book.

PAUL: Sara!

SIR G: Mrs Roger!

GWEN: Mrs Roger!

HARRI: The Welsh Department!

FFIOR: *(embracing her)* Thief! *Ladra!* Oh, I'm so glad!

SIR G: Would it be too much for me to ask for more of that brandy?

SARA: *(serving him cheerfully)* It's good, isn't it? I opened the bottle last night to celebrate my freedom.

PAUL: Sara, you never drank brandy before.

SARA: But last night was a great night, Paul.

FFIOR: May I have a drop too, Sara? I'm feeling quite odd.

GWEN: I never dreamed that the life of the staff was like this.

HARRI: It's more like the West Indies than Wales.

GWEN: I'm beginning to change my mind about marrying a teacher, Harri.

SARA: By the way, Gwen, I got your letter. Thank you for writing it.

GWEN: Letter? . . . . What letter?

SARA: Your letter to me. The letter you lost at the dance.

GWEN: *(fearfully)* I didn't lose a letter at the dance.

SARA: Really?

GWEN: I lost four pounds.

SARA: You didn't know that you also lost a letter?

HARRI: Yes, Gwen. You said that you'd lost four pounds and a private letter you hadn't yet posted from your handbag. Don't you remember?

GWEN: *(turning pale and weak)* I didn't lose a letter. I didn't, I didn't.

SARA: In all fairness, it's an easy thing for you to forget. For that

107

matter, you forgot to put your name to it . . . Sit down, Gwen . . . Are you ill?

GWEN: *(sitting down)* May I have a drop of that brandy?

SARA: Give her a glass, Paul, will you?
(Paul serves her and she drinks.)

HARRI: What is it, Gwen? The strain? This theft after the dance last night?

GWEN: *(trying to control her tears)* Mrs Roger, *you* searched my handbag too?

SARA: No, Gwen dear. I got your letter this morning.

GWEN: I didn't post the letter.

SARA: There wasn't any stamp on it either. Like the last time.

GWEN: So you did search my handbag?

SIR G: I suppose you will acknowledge, Mrs Roger, that your behaviour requires some explanation?

SARA: You should be pleased, Sir Gamaliel.

SIR G: Because no one from the staff is guilty? To be sure, that saves the respectability of the University. But you are the wife of a professor, Mrs Roger . . . It is true that you were in a situation that was a bit exceptional last night. Your future was in danger. Do you think, Mrs Roger, that that can justify — well! What shall I call it? Kleptomania?

SARA: Suppose for a moment, Sir Gamaliel, that you had arrived home last night from London without a penny in your pocket, and you had lost your job, and you were without any supper, and the house was shut in your face —

SIR G: Mrs Roger, I cannot imagine any such thing. The house shut in my face, when I am the principal —
(A clear, light tenor voice is heard from upstairs singing the folk song "Mae gen i dipyn o dŷ bach twt":

> I've got myself a neat little house,
> A neat little house, a neat little house,
> I've got myself a neat little house,
>> With the wind in the door each morning.)

PAUL: Who the devil is upstairs? Who's singing? *(A door is heard closing with a bang.)* There's someone in the house, Sara!

SARA: It's all right. Don't be upset. That's the lodger. He's just had a bath. All lodgers sing after a bath.

PAUL: A lodger you said? What lodger? When did he come?

SARA: Last night.

PAUL: What?

SARA: After you left. I didn't dream that you'd come back this morning.

PAUL: Sara, you're mad!

SARA: I? Not likely! It's a matter of business. Bread and cheese. I have to provide for the future. You'll be in Pisa at Easter, in Florence and Siena.

PAUL: To hell with Florence and Siena! This is my home. Who is this lodger?

SARA: He's a quite pleasant young man and from a good family.

PAUL: Where did you get hold of him? Did he sleep here last night?

SARA: Well, of course he did. I had to have someone with me.

PAUL: With you?

SARA: Did you expect me to sleep by myself?

PAUL: *(at the top of his voice)* He slept with you?

SARA: Does it matter to you?

PAUL: Sara! . . . Sara!

SARA: It will be easier for you to get a divorce.

PAUL: Don't talk nonsense. You know as well as I do that that's over.

SARA: Are you quite sure?

PAUL: Ask her.

SARA: He was in the boys' room. Not on the Harz mountains.

FFIOR: You are a snake, Sara, a snake.

SARA: Men are funny creatures, Ffioretta, as you'll soon learn.

PAUL: Give me a swallow of that brandy, quickly, please.

        (Paul takes a glass and pours brandy and drinks it, and we hear the sound of Sam's feet descending the stairs as he sings)

            Open the door a little crack more,

            A little crack more, a little crack more,

            Open the door a little crack more . . .

        (Sam opens the door and stands in the room and sings the last line:)

            To see the waves on the sea-shore.

SAM: Well! Are there people here? Goodness!

        (Sam is wearing a scarlet dressing gown that belongs to Paul.)

GWEN: Sam!

HARRI: Sam!

FFIOR: Sam!
       (Sir Gamaliel rises to his feet and stares at him, then in a fearful voice:)
SIR G: Samuel! . . . Samuel!
SAM: *(smiling cheerfully but without going to him)* Dad! Gaffer! Presiding at a cocktail-party before eleven in the morning! You haven't changed a bit! And you over sixty years old! Just the same tricks as years ago in Hong-Kong! Brandy, yes? Not martinis? I had no idea that things like this went on in Wales! Here's a very merry meeting!
SIR G: Where did you come from?
SAM: From wandering the face of the earth. Australia first, Italy, Paris, London, then "the land of my fathers".
SIR G: Why?
SAM: Why? Well, "After sampling each spot, its church, lodgings, and beer, / And making love to its maidens" —
HARRI: "After roving, strolling each town" —
SAM: "It's lovely to look towards home."
SIR G: There's no home for you here.
SAM: Do you hear the man, Sara? Shutting the door slap in my face, when I thought that this was *your* home.
SIR G: When did you come?
SAM: On the same train as you, gaffer. I almost asked you to pay for my ticket. But that might have spoiled this happy meeting amidst the staff, with its delightful aroma of brandy.
SIR G: From where?
SAM: From Wandsworth. Have you been there? . . . No? I was one of three in a room that was somewhat confining, and I said to myself, "How many hirelings has my father . . . ?" You know the rest? And here I am.
SIR G: You are the thief?
SAM: Which job are you referring to now? Melbourne or Soho?
SIR G: Last night at the College dance?
SAM: That trifle? It isn't worth talking about. Some twenty-four pounds and a few papers.
SIR G: I must apologize to you, Mrs Roger.
SARA: Your father wanted to send for the police, Sam, but Ffioretta stopped him.

SAM: Ffioretta! Well done, my girl! Come here and give me a kiss.
        (She embraces and kisses him and he holds her.)
FFIOR: *Samuele mio!*
SAM: Who was right, girl?
FFIOR: You were right, Sam.
SAM: Have you learned your lesson?
FFIOR: Yes, Sam.
SAM: I have some further lessons for you.
FFIOR: Darling!
        (He releases her and turns towards Sara.)
SAM: Where did you put my coat, Sara?
SARA: In the airing cupboard upstairs.
SAM: Was it dirty?
SARA: It's been cleaned.
SAM: I have papers in it.
SARA: I have your father's cheque book.
SAM: Sara! You picked my pocket while I was in the bath! Thief!
SARA: That's what your father called me.
SAM: And I thought I'd stumbled on a simple-minded little
        woman last night wandering the streets after midnight!
        Upon my life! And what about the money?
SARA: The money is in your coat pocket. *You* can pay the four
        pounds back to Gwen.
SAM: To Gwen? No no no! I have a quite handy little letter from
        Gwen that's worth more than four pounds. Isn't it, Gwen?
SARA: How much is it worth?
SAM: These students can afford it. Say three pounds a month for a
        year until graduation. Or the little letter will go to the
        Principal, and a copy to the College Registrar. The Principal
        hasn't had a letter from me for quite some time.
SARA: It was a letter to me.
SAM: Sara dear, everything is in common between us since last
        night. I hid the letter in the lining of my coat.
SARA: Yes. I mended the lining.
SAM: What? And took the letter?
SARA: And put it on the fire.
SAM: Burning good money! A sinful thing, Sara, sinful! Isn't it,
        Dad? Women have no conscience when it comes to money.
SARA: Don't say that in front of my husband.

SAM: Paul? The famous Paul? The great professor? The subject of the eloquent letter!
         (Gwen gives a low cry like a moan and slips into a faint. Harri holds her and Sara runs to help.)
SARA: Bring her into the next room so she can lie on the sofa.
         (Sara and Harri carry Gwen out.)
PAUL: Would you like a drop of brandy, Sam, to drink to your father's health?
SAM: Sir, it's a pleasure to meet a Welsh professor who's so civilized. The influence of Florence, right?
FFIOR: *(with contempt)* U-w-d!
PAUL: *(raising his glass to her)* Ice cream.
SAM: So it is in this world: Between porridge and ice-cream the romance of love is drowned. I saw the same thing happen in Wandsworth at breakfast time: two lovers like David and Jonathan forever fighting over a plate of porridge.
SIR G: I find your blasphemy distasteful.
SAM: And you an unbeliever, Dad! But there it is, I've heard that all the unbelievers in Wales today go to church or chapel, for the sake of saving the Welsh language.
FFIOR: You didn't get that dressing gown in Wandsworth, Sam.
SAM: Sara let me borrow this. Posh, isn't it?
FFIOR: It's from Florence. A present I gave to Paul.
SAM: I see. That's why Sara chucked it to me.
FFIOR: Chucked it?
SAM: As if it were a shirt in Wandsworth.
FFIOR: You're quite at home with Sara.
SAM: Contented. Like a member of the staff. A typical Welsh household, bi-lingual and two-faced. Isn't it, Paul?
PAUL: You can keep that dressing gown to remember Sara.
FFIOR: No you can't!
SAM: Oho! Jealousy, my sweet?
SIR G: *(having made up his mind)* Samuel!
SAM: Father . . . Speak: your servant is listening.
SIR G: You haven't come here to ask about my health.
SAM: I did ask. The report was depressing: completely recovered.
SIR G: What is your business here?
SAM: Must you ask? I have only one business, like everybody else.

SIR G: Very well. You had better come back to the house with me.

SAM: No, there's no need for that, Dad. Your cheque book is very conveniently here with Sara.

SIR G: Have you no shame?

SAM: At this moment, Dad, these two birds, taken in adultery, are the only members of the College staff who know of my existence . . . If you put me off, the whole college will get to know.

FFIOR: The good name of the University, *caro rettore*, I beg you.

PAUL: You've just been made a knight, Sir Gamaliel! I beg you.

SAM: For the old folks at home, Dad, I beg you.

FFIOR: For the good name of the college and the council.

PAUL: For the Prime Minister who submitted your name for a knighthood.

SAM: In memory of my mother, Dad, in memory of my mother.

SIR G: Samuel, you turn my stomach.

SAM: That's the only pleasure I have left, Dad.

SIR G: How much?

SAM: A thousand pounds.

SIR G: Impossible . . . You had a thousand pounds the last time. I paid for a three year course so that you could take your degree in agriculture at Melbourne, and then start on the ranch.

SAM: That was nine years ago.

SIR G: You didn't get your degree. You never saw the ranch.

SAM: Be fair now. I lost four hundred on the horses in Melbourne. Today I have an infallible system.

SIR G: An infallible system! And you end up in Wandsworth.

SAM: That's where I learned the system. From a stockbroker.

SIR G: Samuel, I am sixty-two years old. I only have three more years. Then this blackmail will be over. I will live on my pension and you won't get a brass farthing.

SAM: Six hundred.

SIR G: If you won't be reasonable I can retire quite comfortably this summer.

SAM: Five hundred.

SIR G: Things have changed, my boy. I have been living as principal at this college for eight years. I have had experience, you see, with the college council, with the academic staff, I'm

	accustomed to every type of pressure and black-mail, I've lived and lived successfully with rascals just like you.
SAM:	Four hundred. That's my final offer, Dad, four hundred.
SIR G:	You won't get that either. I'll give you a cheque for a hundred pounds today. Then you will have a hundred pounds a year until I retire, on the condition that you do not come back to England or Wales while I am principal. If you do, you won't get a penny, I will call for the police and retire.
SAM:	*(shouting)* Sara! *(Sara comes in)* . . . Where is the gaffer's cheque book?
SARA:	Under the telephone.
	(She gets it and gives it to the Principal.)
SIR G:	Do you have an account in the bank? — in red ink?
SAM:	In Melbourne, Dad. Red ink for six years. Cheques bouncing back like tennis balls.
SIR G:	Then how do I make out a cheque to you?
SAM:	To Miss Ffioretta Davies. Ffioretta and I intend to meet in Pisa during the Easter holidays.
FFIOR:	*(embracing him)* Sam! You're an angel, Sam!
SAM:	Picking pockets and making love.
FFIOR:	Pisa at Easter!
SAM:	Palermo, Napoli!
FFIOR:	Experiences of love and artistic experiences together!
SAM:	And the casino at Monte Carlo! An infallible system!
SIR G:	*(handing her the cheque)* Then here is the cheque, Miss Davies.
FFIOR:	*(putting it in her bag and taking out a letter and placing it in front of Sir Gamaliel)* And here is the letter, *caro rettore*.
SIR G:	Letter?
FFIOR:	A letter of recommendation for me for the position in London. Already typed on the college stationery. All you need to do is sign your name.
SIR G:	Blackmail again, is that it?
FFIOR:	But of course, *caro*.
SIR G:	*(reading)* "Miss Ffioretta Davies, daughter of a distinguished Welsh writer who was for many years British consul at Florence — . . ." the usual lies, I suppose?
FFIOR:	One or two unusual ones as well.

SIR G: *(signing his name)* It's sure to succeed. The Principal is a bachelor.

SAM: Come to the bank with me, Ffioretta. I must get my coat. *(They go out on the left, arm in arm.)*

PAUL: Is there anything left after breakfast, Sara?

SARA: There's a plate of porridge in a dish on the stove.

PAUL: *Uwd!* Thank goodness for a Welsh home, Sir Gamaliel. I have a lecture at twelve.
(Paul exits on the left.)

SARA: You owe me a debt, Sir Gamaliel.

SIR G: *(going to her)* A rather large debt . . . Is there a way to pay it?

SARA: I don't know whether you'll agree . . . It would be a quite sensible thing to appoint Paul Vice-Chancellor of the College next year.

SIR G: A splendid idea, Mrs. Roger. Then we can keep today's troubles and last night's a secret in our own little circle. I will make sure that the Council appoints him . . . And what about these two students? They have heard things . . .

SARA: I will take care of them like a mother. They're nice children.

SIR G: Yes, aren't they? May I ask you where you acquired your knack?

SARA: I never went to college.

SIR G: That's it. You had a chance to grow up . . . Yes. yes, the University in Wales is a nursery school.

SARA: Especially the departments of Welsh.

SIR G: It's a pity you're married, Mrs Roger. Since I'm a widower, you would make a proper helpmate to a principal.

SARA: Sam will come back within two years.

SIR G: Stay here to help me, Mrs Roger.

SARA: We'll arrange things very well, Sir Gamaliel. I will silence Sam, and Paul will slip quietly into your place as Principal . . . Agreed?
(They walk together into the garden . . . Gwen and Harri enter from the left)

HARRI: Everybody's gone . . . Aren't the staff meetings interesting?

GWEN: I'll come with you to Galway this summer, Harri.

HARRI: Galway? Oh no, I've changed my mind. I want to go to Florence. It's better preparation for a principal.

115

GWEN: *(taking his arm)* Sir G said I'd make a suitable wife for a
principal . . .
(And they go out through the garden.)

THE END

TOMORROW'S WALES

(Cymru Fydd, 1967)

My prefaces to the preceding two plays should also be used as background for this one (including its title), and supplemented with the following information.

Cymdeithas Yr Iaith Gymraeg, The Welsh Language Society, was formed in 1962, largely as a result of Saunders Lewis' speech on "The Fate of the Language" and in the absence of a positive response to this by The Welsh Nationalist Party (*Plaid Cymru*). The speech declared that "the Welsh language can be saved" from what is otherwise certain destruction only through a campaign of civil disobedience, by making it "impossible for the business of local and central government to continue without using Welsh". Welsh-speaking university students in particular joined *Cymdeithas*; the play refers to an actual incident resulting from a demonstration in the town of Dolgellau in 1965.

The play also alludes to the dam and reservoir constructed by the Corporation of Liverpool at Tryweryn in North Wales. The dam was authorized by Act of Parliament in 1957 and officially opened in 1963, despite the protests of 125 Welsh local authorities and of trade union branches and religious and cultural organizations against this flooding of the Tryweryn valley and the consequent dispersion of the Welsh-language population of Capel Celyn, a village that for centuries had been a vital centre of Welsh culture. The incident exemplified for Welsh nationalists the powerlessness of Wales without a parliament of its own to protect its basic interests as a community against the use of its natural resources for English industry. (There is also an oblique reference to this incident in *Esther*.)

I have retained "Dewi" as the form of the central character's name in my script, but in any production of the play for primarily non-Welsh audiences consideration should be given to calling him "David", to retain the association of his name with Saint David, *Dewi Sant*, the patron saint of Wales.

CHARACTERS

The Reverend John Rhys
Dora, his wife
Dewi, their son
Bet Edward
Constable Jones
Inspector Evans
Two other policemen

Scene: The parlour of a minister's house in a village in North Wales.

ACT I

*The parlour in the minister's house, about seven o'clock in the evening.
The fire is lit in the grate and the electric light is on in the room, since it is
an evening in November. Dora, the minister's wife, enters, dressed to go
out. She is in early middle age, but her hair is white. She looks around,
tends to the fire, then puts out the light and is turning to go out when the
telephone (stage left) rings.*

DORA: *(answering the phone)* Tan-y-fron two-three-seven . . . No,
he isn't . . . The minister's just left for the society . . . Yes,
he'll be back here within an hour . . . What? . . . Am I by
myself? . . . Yes, at the moment, I'm about to start for the
society too . . . Why? . . . Who's calling? . . . What name do
I tell my husband? . . . Well, if you wish to see him come here
about eight . . . You won't give your name? . . . Very well,
about eight o'clock . . .
*(She puts the telephone down and gazes into the fire for a rather
long moment in meditation. There is a window at the back of
the room on the right side that opens onto the garden. It is
suddenly raised. We see in the half-gloom a young man in a
dark green mackintosh putting his leg over the windowsill and
climbing into the parlour. Dora gives ₐa long frightened
scream.)*

DEWI: Sh, Mam, sh! . . . It's me. Dewi!
DORA: What?
DEWI: Dewi. It's me.
DORA: Dewi?
DEWI: Yes. Here I am!
DORA: Oh dear, dear. Oh, I had a fright.

DEWI: Everything's fine, Mam.

DORA: It isn't fine, it's far from being fine. Nothing is fine. Leaping at me through the window like that . . . Wait till I put on the light. *(She moves towards the light switch, but he is there more quickly and pushes her away.)*

DEWI: Damn it, Mam! Be sensible.

DORA: Why? What's wrong?

DEWI: People could see me. Draw the curtains across the windows first. *(He shuts and locks the window and she pulls the cord that closes the heavy curtains. Then she turns on the light. They face each other.)*

DORA: Dewi!

DEWI: Well, Mam, how are things?

DORA: *(sitting on the edge of a chair)* Oh Dewi!

DEWI: You don't have a kiss for me? Not a word of welcome? Just "Oh Dewi!"?

DORA: Bring me a little water from the kitchen.
(He goes to the kitchen through the door on the left. She over-comes her distress with a great effort and takes off her coat and hat and gloves.)

DEWI: *(bringing her a small glass of water)* I'm sorry I frightened you like that, Mam.

DORA: *(after sipping)* I'll be all right in a moment.

DEWI: You were starting for the meeting?

DORA: About to start . . . Did you see your father?

DEWI: No.

DORA: He just left the house. How is it you didn't see him on the road?

DEWI: How is he?

DORA: What would you expect?

DEWI: Yes, I suppose. He's stayed in the church?

DORA: So far.

DEWI: I wouldn't want to be a cause of him leaving it.

DORA: It's rather late for you to begin worrying about your father. Was it to show your godliness you came in through the window?

DEWI: *(a short laugh)* It's good to see you've kept your old tartness, Mam.

DORA: Retching isn't tartness.

DEWI: And you wouldn't want people to see me knocking on the
          front door. I'll bet the bell still isn't fixed, is it? And the
          window unlocked as usual.

DORA: *(putting the glass down and turning to him)* Where did you
          come from?

DEWI: From there, of course . . . Where else?

DORA: From the prison?

DEWI: From the prison.

DORA: Are you free?

DEWI: Yes . . . free . . . now.

DORA: But how? You were given twelve months. Why didn't we
          have notice? . . . Why didn't you send a message? . . . Your
          father has sold the car, but we could have had a taxi to fetch
          you.

DEWI: It was all rather sudden. There was no time to send word.

DORA: Why? When were you released?

DEWI: This morning.

DORA: The governor . . . ?

DEWI: *(laughing)* No, not exactly. But the governor was a help.

DORA: Then what happened? I didn't know such a thing was
          possible.

DEWI: Everything's possible . . . with luck!

DORA: With luck?

DEWI: I wasn't released.

DORA: You weren't? What happened?

DEWI: I walked out . . . Quite simple.

DORA: *(on her feet in anguish)* Dewi! . . . You didn't escape?

DEWI: Yes . . . I escaped! . . . I escaped!

DORA: Do they know? The officers?

DEWI: They're sure to, by now.

DORA: When was this?

DEWI: This morning. About eleven. You didn't hear the six o'clock
          news on the radio?

DORA: No. I don't listen to any of it now . . . How did you come
          home?

DEWI: There was a thick mist. I reached the highway and had a ride
          with a lorry right away.

DORA: A lorry? From the other side of Gloucester? All the way here?

DEWI: He was taking cement to Pwllheli. A Welshman. A decent fellow.

DORA: The police will be after you.

DEWI: They're sure to be. That's the sort they are, you see.

DORA: No one stopped the lorry for questioning?

DEWI: Questioning?

DORA: That's what they do, according to the papers, when someone escapes from prison.

DEWI: Yes, don't they? No, no one stopped us. He was a first-class driver.

DORA: They'll come here, they'll come here after you.

DEWI: That's why I came through the garden and the window. For fear Jones, the village policeman, has had warning.

DORA: Of course he'll have had warning.

DEWI: Well, the manse here is a bit apart, not in the middle of the village . . . Does he still have that motor-bike?

DORA: Who?

DEWI: Jones the policeman.

DORA: You're talking hatefully, like someone who's become a hardened thief and murderer.

DEWI: That's what I am, a professional thief. Not a murderer though, up to now, as far as I know.

DORA: You can't hide here, Dewi.

DEWI: Why not?

DORA: Because your father is a minister of the Gospel.

DEWI: *(smiling)* That's why I can hide here. That's why I came here. Dad is respectable and honest. The police and the justices all sympathize with him in his disgrace and tribulation. He did the most to prove that I was guilty, helped the police the best he could.

DORA: For you. To have your sentence reduced. And he succeeded.

DEWI: All right. Perhaps he had other reasons too, a bit different. I don't blame him for that. But now all he needs to do is say he hasn't seen me, and there's an end to it. They'll never search the house of such an honest minister. His word will be enough. I'll be safe here for a bit, Mam.

DORA: There's only one place you'll be safe, my boy.

DEWI: Where?

DORA: In prison, completing your sentence. Then you'll be a free man and can start living again.

DEWI: *(after a short laugh)* The way of the cross, right?

DORA: It's a bitter way, not only for you. But that's the only way. I'm your mother. You are the only fruit of my womb. My bowels tremble for you day and night . . . Your father's head is bowed like an old man and he's barely middle-aged. And I'm . . . as you see me. But going back to prison, giving yourself up to the police, that's the only way to freedom, this very night.

(The telephone rings. Dora turns to pick it up and answer. Dewi grasps her and stops her. The telephone rings between Dewi's sentences as he talks.)

DEWI: You're at the society, Mam, . . . Listening to the experiences of the saints . . . You hear them? . . . There's no one in the house to answer the telephone . . . *(Ringing)* O where is my wandering boy tonight . . .

(The telephone stops).

DORA: *(freeing herself, sharply)* Hold your tongue!

DEWI: *(laughing)* Don't make a tragedy out of my coming home, Mam. After all I'm breaking up the monotony of the life of the chapel and the manse. You don't have a television set, but I'm almost as good.

DORA: There was someone inquiring on the telephone just before you climbed through the window.

DEWI: I know. I was listening.

DORA: So they know that you came towards home.

DEWI: When someone escapes the police always watch his home. It's a rule. I knew that.

DORA: I'm glad you came home. Home-sickness, *hiraeth*, will be an excuse to some extent . . . *(Dewi laughs softly)* . . . Why are you laughing? What did I say that's so amusing?

DEWI: It isn't important, Mam dear. But that word "*hiraeth*". I haven't heard it for centuries. To my generation it's a meaningless word, something out of the Welsh poetry book long ago in school.

DORA: The most sensible thing for you, the best thing for your own good, is to phone the police yourself right now to say that you're here and ask them to come here.

DEWI: *(becoming serious)* I don't want to be hateful. But I need to be able to stay here quietly all night tonight.

DORA: My dear boy, your father will be here in a moment. The first thing he'll do once he's heard your story will be to phone the police in town. You know that. And you know that's what will be best for you too.

DEWI: He won't be able to phone tonight.

DORA: *(without any fear, but coldly)* Do I understand you correctly? Are you threatening to raise your hand to your father?

DEWI: There's more than one way to skin a cat.

DORA: For example?

DEWI: You, not I, will keep Dad from phoning.

DORA: I've never in my life tried to keep your father from acting according to his conscience.

DEWI: You can change his conscience.

DORA: How? . . . Why?

DEWI: You'll tell him that I need to have at least one night of sleep without trembling in fear. I need to be able to take my clothes off. I need to be able to go to bed without having to listen for every squeak in the darkness.

DORA: You're not by yourself?

DEWI: There are two of us. Every prison in Britain is like that now.

DORA: Like that . . . how?

DEWI: My partner is a thirty-year-old boxer from Stepney. We're locked together in a small, high, narrow cell from six every afternoon till six every morning, twelve hours together, like Adam and Eve in Paradise. What the English call "a marriage of convenience".

DORA: *(with a cry)* Dewi! What are you saying?

DEWI: Just sharing a bit of my experience on a society night . . . "A privilege, a privilege is fellowship" . . . you know?

DORA: Do things like that really happen?

DEWI: That isn't your idea of prison, Mam? Did you think it was a Welsh nursery school? Or a monastery? . . . *(Dora shakes her head in pain)* . . . A prison is Sodom and Gomorrah, and the walls and the locked doors make sure that there's no choice and no refusing.

DORA: Why wasn't there a way for you to change your cell?

125

DEWI: *(with a bitter laugh)* Change my cell? I could, probably, — just go to the governor and complain.

DORA: And why not?

DEWI: Complain to the governor? . . . *(A short laugh)* You don't know what a funny idea that is. There are things I can't tell you that happen on parade there at six every morning. Boys who've complained to the governor have gone straight to the asylum from the punishments there . . . I wouldn't need to change my cell twice.

DORA: You mean to frighten me — you're succeeding.

DEWI: Did you think I would be purified in prison? That I would go back afterwards to college to lead the youth of Wales in a new religious revival?

DORA: I had no notion. Prison to me was something I read about in the newspaper before this happened. I was afraid that prison could embitter a boy like you, turn you into an enemy of your father and your mother and everybody. I've been praying for these last three months that it wouldn't happen . . . It has happened . . . But I didn't imagine that prison could contaminate and pollute and prostitute and destroy boys' manhood.

DEWI: A country village in Welsh-speaking Wales can do that too, you know.

DORA: Not everyone in a village is corrupt.

DEWI: Not everyone in prison is corrupt either. Half of them are half-wits, simpletons, not all there. The prison hospital is full of boys who have swallowed needles or sometimes half a scissors while sewing bags. They go to the hospital then, and wait until the needle pricks. Then an operation. A high old time.

DORA: That is also an escape.

DEWI: And that's what I did this morning. As the son of the manse and the child of the Sunday school I walked out. And I'm not going back there like a little lamb so that Dad can see himself phoning the police like Abraham going to sacrifice Isaac.

DORA: You don't know your father at all.

DEWI: That's very true. It's impossible. It's exceptional for a father and a son ever to understand each other. Between one's birth and the other's the language has changed.

DORA: There's one thing tormenting me now, Dewi.

DEWI: Only one?

DORA: I don't know at this moment whether you *can* tell the truth any more.

DEWI: Mam dear, you're taking me right back to philosophy class in college.

DORA: How so?

DEWI: What is the truth? The thing you believe at the moment?

DORA: Or the thing you say at the moment?

DEWI: Saying it and believing it perhaps, saying it in order to believe it.

DORA: I don't know at this moment whether you're telling the true reason why you escaped from prison, or if it's all a trick to snare me into helping you.

DEWI: *(after laughing)* That's pretty good. The fact is that you have too much brain to behave like a mother.

DORA: I'm only forty-two years old, my boy, and my hair is already white because of you.

DEWI: *(uncomfortably)* Have you such a thing as food in the house?

DORA: When did you last eat?

DEWI: Breakfast, at seven this morning.

DORA: I have hot rice pudding and an apple tart — that, with tea and bread and butter?

DEWI: Here?

DORA: Upstairs. Your father will be here any moment. Your bed and the room are the way they were. I'll put a candle on the small table by the bed. Just draw the curtains and don't turn on the electric light, no one can see you or see your shadow. *(Dora exits to the kitchen through the door on the left. Dewi walks hesitantly back and forth; then, at last, with a determined step, he picks up the telephone and dials, and listens . . .)*

DEWI: Bet! Hello! . . . It's me . . . *(smiling at the girl's surprise)* . . . Home for a night or two, I'll explain later . . . Listen; is there a chance you can come here? . . . Don't come along the main road. There'll be cops around there. Come across the fields and through the back garden . . . I'll be at the back door waiting for you . . . Mam will be in bed about ten and Dad in his study. Come then . . . We need to get things clear between us, that's why I came here . . . No more in case there are ears listening . . . Till tonight!

(He puts the telephone down. He walks again, too casually. Dora comes to the door.)

DORA: Your supper is ready upstairs, and towels for you to wash. Go on now — don't dawdle. I heard your father's step.

(And he goes out with her . . . The Reverend John Rhys comes in, looks anxiously around, then calls)

JOHN: Dora! . . . Dora!

DORA: *(in the doorway)* Hello!

JOHN: Are you ill?

DORA: Not now. I'm all right.

JOHN: I missed you at the society and came here and saw your things here and the glass of water there.

DORA: I had a moment of dizziness when I was about to start, and I thought it was best to stay home.

JOHN: Certainly. Has it gone?

DORA: I think so.

JOHN: I'll take my coat off before I sit down.

(He goes out through the middle door and Dora places a chair for him to sit near the fire on the front right, so that he may face the audience. She takes up her knitting. And he returns.)

DORA: You're back remarkably soon.

JOHN: Yes. It's as well you didn't come.

DORA: Why?

JOHN: Four people came to the society. One was simple-minded Hugh; John Evans, who's over eighty; and those two old dears Jane and Cathrin. And they're not like everybody else.

DORA: Not one deacon?

JOHN: Not one.

DORA: What did you do?

JOHN: Conducted family prayers, and finished in ten minutes.

DORA: In that case I'm sorry I was missing.

JOHN: You always like the homely things.

DORA: Do you remember that week of holidays we had near Dulverton the spring after we were married?

JOHN: I remember it very well. A week of fishing without a care in the world. What about it?

DORA: It came into my mind just now how every living man in that village was reeling drunk on Saturday night.

JOHN: And the women collected their men from the taverns to guide them safely home at ten o'clock. It was a strange and amusing sight, more amusing than sad I suppose.

DORA: And the next morning, Sunday morning, I went to the parish church for the morning service.

JOHN: I remember that too. And I went for a stroll along the banks of the river Exe and saw the biggest salmon I ever saw swimming in a river, the king of salmon.

DORA: The river was more full than the church. There wasn't a living person at the service except the vicar and the sexton making the responses and myself as the congregation.

JOHN: Rural England, you see. The small country villages in Devonshire are stranger than anything in Wales, more primitive.

DORA: I had a chat afterwards with the vicar. He was perfectly happy, went home cheerfully. The service had been held. Worship had been given for the whole parish, though only three were there. It was offering worship regularly for the parish that was important. He didn't imagine for a moment that it was necessary for him to give up the church and resign because none of the wardens was there, no one but the sexton half-asleep and me.

(John looks at her in surprise and then laughs heartily.)

JOHN: Dora, Dora, I haven't said one word about giving up the church, not one word.

DORA: Don't talk nonsense. Resignation was written all over your face.

JOHN: You're a witch, woman, a witch. I dismissed the society tonight in ten minutes and I walked home constructing a letter to the deacons to say that I will sever my connection with the church at the end of the year . . . That's what's best. That's what's necessary.

DORA: In spite of the godly vicar in Devonshire?

JOHN: It wasn't the vicar who emptied the church there. But here, I'm the one responsible, I'm the cause of the empty chapel.

DORA: And why you?

JOHN: You know why. If I can't raise my own child as a moral character, what right have I to go into the pulpit? What right have I to counsel and question at the society? That's what the deacons are whispering to each other, and keeping away on purpose. I must resign so that they and the ordinary members as well can return to the means of grace.

DORA: Do you remember Dewi's age?

JOHN: He's twenty-two. The trial and the verdict were on his birthday. How could I not remember?

DORA: Then you're not responsible. He was at college for four years, and came home only on holidays. You don't wish to ask the professor to resign?

JOHN: Preaching the Gospel isn't a professor's job. He isn't responsible either for the life or the morals of the students. I'm responsible, and I've failed in my prayers, in my example, in my son . . . Do you know that mounting the steps of the pulpit is like going into the dock at the assizes for me? I'm there, in the dock with Dewi, facing the judge and the jurors every time I announce a hymn to be sung. Dora, Dewi is my failure. I'm the one who's guilty.

DORA: In that case, John, you have no right to put aside the care of the church.

JOHN: What is it you're saying?

DORA: Every preacher should enter the pulpit in that spirit. The guilty preacher is the one with the right to preach. Otherwise he'd be unbearable.

JOHN: I can't preach now.

DORA: I can listen to you preach now without being afraid for you.

JOHN: You're arguing that I shouldn't write to the deacons?

DORA: You know, if you resign, they can't afford another minister. You give your salary back to them every year.

JOHN: You're the one does that, not I. That's the only reason they haven't asked me to resign. It's your money we live on.

DORA: And you know, John, given that you resign, the meeting wouldn't be one jot more full, or the Sunday morning service. It's like that through the whole country. Our religion is something that's dying.

(John rises and walks agitatedly up and down. Then he stands and asks her:)

JOHN: Dora, do you think . . . ? Every night I think, — he's sleeping, I suppose, there in his cell?

DORA: Who knows? Chances are he'll manage to sleep tonight.

JOHN: I heard Williams Parry say that being locked in a cell was the worst of all fears to him. Claustrophobia, you know? That would keep me miserable at night too. I can understand a person being unable to bear it.

DORA: Being locked in by oneself would be a kind of security for a person. I can think of a worse fear, to find myself locked in at night with someone who terrifies me.

JOHN: The governor there, according to what I've heard, is a rather progressive and humane man. After the first three months of probation some of the criminals are allowed to go to work outside the prison walls, with only one guard in charge of them. That could save many a man from losing his mind.

DORA: Would you like some supper?

JOHN: I'd really rather do without supper if it wouldn't upset you. Didn't you say you had an apple tart and pudding?

DORA: It doesn't matter. I thought I could tempt you to eat. I just remembered — there was someone on the telephone asking for you?

JOHN: Who was it?

DORA: He refused to give his name. He wanted to call tonight. I told him you would be free about eight o'clock.

JOHN: I'm not in a mood to have a chat with anyone.

DORA: He wasn't one of the deacons, I knew by the voice.

JOHN: Sh!

DORA: What did you hear?

JOHN: A motorbike.

DORA: In the lane?

JOHN: Yes . . . Here he is! . . . *(We hear a heavy knocking on the door of the house)* . . . We're used to that knocking.

DORA: I'll go.
(Exit Dora, through the middle door. She comes back and opens the door for Constable Jones who is carrying his motor-cycle helmet under one arm.)

JONES: Good evening, sir. I'm sorry to disturb you.

JOHN: You're the one who phoned?

JONES: No, sir. The inspector from town. Then I received an order to come here with a message.

JOHN: There's only one thing that can bring you here, — my son.

JONES: That's it, sir. I'm sorry.

JOHN: Sit down.

JONES: For a minute or two, sir.

JOHN: Bad news?

JONES: Well, yes.

JOHN: Is he ill?

JONES: No. He's missing . . . he's escaped.

JOHN: Dewi! . . . Escaped? How?

JONES: A party from the prison, those with a three month record of good behaviour, was working on one of the houses outside the prison. Your son was one of them for three days. There was no trouble for two days. This morning there was a thick mist over the whole district. Dewi Rhys disappeared in the mist. It was close to one o'clock, when the party returned to the prison, before they knew that he was missing.

JOHN: The imbecile! Oh Dewi! Dewi!

JONES: That isn't all, sir. That isn't the worst.

JOHN: Have the police caught him?

JONES: They're fairly sure of doing that tonight or tomorrow.

JOHN: What direction did he take? Do they know?

JONES: There's a middle-aged man, a commercial traveller, in hospital — he's been hurt, he's had a pretty bad blow on the head and cracked his skull. He was found lying on the side of the highway.

DORA: Dewi? . . . Yes? Dewi?

JONES: Yes, ma'am.

JOHN: Is the man in danger?

JONES: He'll get over it, according to the doctor. He was able to tell the policeman at his bedside what happened.

JOHN: Tell us.

JONES: He had stopped because of the mist. Then because the battery of his car was somewhat low he took the crank to the front of the car to start the engine. It didn't go right away, he says. He was out of breath, and then a young man, he didn't know from where, comes across the road to him and offers help. And he gave him the crank, and he started the engine

132

very quickly. He turned to thank the lad and had a blow on his head with the crank, and he fell to the ground like that, he didn't know any more. He was groaning terribly and coming to when the police found him.

JOHN: And the lad was Dewi?

JONES: Positively. The traveller's description fits. Later, this afternoon, the car was in Kington getting petrol. The driver was a young lad in a dark green mackintosh, the garage man said. The traveller had left his wallet with his money in his coat on the front seat of the car.

JOHN: Kington? Near the Welsh border?

JONES: Kington is on the direct route here, Mr Rhys.

JOHN: The police will be watching the road?

JONES: Of course. The case is much more serious than escaping from prison. Robbery with G.B.H.

DORA: What is G.B.H.?

JONES: Grievous Bodily Harm. The sentence can be four or five years.

JOHN: The sentence isn't what's important tonight. The only thing of any importance is to get hold of the boy and put him in the hands of the police at once, before he gets into worse trouble.

JONES: That's our assignment, sir.

JOHN: The traveller is recovering?

JONES: That's what we heard.

JOHN: At least, he isn't a murderer.

JONES: If he comes here, can we depend on you to ring the inspector, sir?

JOHN: Do you doubt me, Constable?

JONES: Not for a minute, sir. You were very honest with us when he got into trouble earlier. But I have a duty to warn you that giving him refuge would be a crime. It could mean three months in prison.

JOHN: My dear Jones, don't tempt me. That could be a haven for me.

JONES: *(rising and taking his helmet)* I'm heartily sorry for you, Mr Rhys. This is no pleasure for us either.

JOHN: If he comes here, he won't come with the car.

JONES: He won't bring the car into the village or within five miles of

133

the village. He'll come across the fields and through the back garden, the way the village children come to steal your apples, Mrs Rhys.

(John accompanies the policeman through the middle door. Dora stands motionless, controlling her inner turmoil. John comes back through the door on the left.)

DORA: Has he gone?

JOHN: Yes.

DORA: He won't go far.

JOHN: Not for a spell.

DORA: He'll be watching the house.

JOHN: All night.

DORA: All night?

JOHN: Taking turns with another policeman.

DORA: Like a siege.

JOHN: Like a siege . . . *(Pause)*

DORA: And yet, this is his home. This is where he'll expect to find refuge.

JOHN: Dora?

DORA: Well?

JOHN: I went into the kitchen just now.

DORA: Why?

JOHN: I wanted a drop of water.

DORA: Of course.

JOHN: On the edge of the sink . . .

DORA: Yes?

JOHN: There was a pudding dish . . . and the dish for apple tart.

DORA: I put them there to be washed.

JOHN: Yes . . . Dora?

DORA: Well?

JOHN: Where is he?

DORA: Upstairs . . . finishing his supper.

(John paces the room)

JOHN: Why didn't you tell me?

DORA: Tell you when?

JOHN: When I came back. When we were chatting about the chapel. Before the policeman called.

DORA: Because I was expecting the policeman to call. He said eight o'clock. It wasn't right to tell you before that.

JOHN: Why? . . . Dora, why?

DORA: Because you'd have to answer the policeman, not I.

JOHN: Weren't you afraid?

DORA: John dear, for five months now I've slept with fear every night. Fear is part of our lives.

JOHN: When did he arrive?

DORA: I had put out the light to follow you to the society, and in he climbed through the window.

JOHN: He's used to breaking in.

DORA: He was very much on his high horse.

JOHN: Where is the car he had?

DORA: It was from the policeman I first heard of the car.

JOHN: You knew how he came here?

DORA: He had his story. A romantic story. Not the policeman's story.

JOHN: To Dewi there's no difference at all between true and false. That's how he took honours in philosophy.

DORA: We must be thankful that traveller's still alive.

JOHN: I thought we had reached the bottom, that it couldn't get worse.

DORA: There's no bottom to misery. Perhaps tomorrow we'll see tonight as almost heaven.

JOHN: "One heaven alone is sure — the days gone by."

DORA: When he was a child.

JOHN: And such a dear child, so cheerful . . . And full of mischief.

DORA: Racing wildly through his prayers at my knee.

JOHN: The law and the police know nothing of that.

DORA: And he doesn't remember it either.

JOHN: No, he doesn't remember any part of his life. I can't understand that.

DORA: Because he's still a child. A child has only today. All Dewi has is today.

JOHN: . . . And we have to face tomorrow.

DORA: Yes . . . Tomorrow . . . Not tonight.

JOHN: Tonight, Dora. Now. It won't pay us to put it off. It will be harder tomorrow than tonight. We must put first things first, and do what's right. Otherwise we're lost.

DORA: Lost? I'm lost already, lost forever, lost like Dewi.

JOHN: I'll phone now.

(He moves towards the telephone but she stands confronting him)

DORA: No, John, not tonight.

JOHN: Dora dear, don't be insane. There's no choice.

DORA: Yes, there's a choice.

JOHN: It's our duty.

DORA: Duty to whom, John? . . . Duty to whom?

JOHN: To the law . . . to honesty . . . No, that's not it at all. To Dewi himself, to save him.

DORA: Thank you for saying that, John. We're still together. To me the rules of society and the law of the land don't matter now . . . We've stopped being respectable. We have a chance to be human.

JOHN: Hiding him, Dora, would add more to his sentence.

DORA: I've promised, given my word, that he can sleep safely tonight.

JOHN: You don't seriously think he escaped to get a night's sleep?

DORA: *(squeezing her hands in despair)* I can't tell you. I can't name it. It's too dreadful.

JOHN: Do you believe him?

DORA: John, it's necessary to believe him, even in his lies. There's no other way to reach him.

JOHN: You're right. I'll go up and get him to give himself up to the police. Tonight. Now.

(But the centre door is opened and Dewi stands there in a clean suit and an open shirt, smoking a cigarette like a roughneck.)

DEWI: Well, have you settled my fate?

JOHN: *(smiling)* Settled your fate? Dewi, Dewi, don't blaspheme.

DEWI: *(moving away from him and laughing)* Pretty good, Dad. A thoroughly Calvinist answer. And I was afraid our meeting would be rather difficult.

JOHN: You from the jail, me from the society, we've both made our escape. Your mother is urging me to go back too.

DEWI: By all means, Dad. It would be a sinful thing to give up the church.

JOHN: That's your opinion? Escape — you know? — is such a temptation.

136

DEWI: But after all, you hold the meeting, it doesn't hold you.

JOHN: I don't know. If I'm being held, then most likely it does hold me. If I escape, perhaps I won't be held.

DEWI: That's exactly my experience, Dad, — if I escape, perhaps I won't be held.

JOHN: Philosopher and theologian agree! It's strange how quickly two generations come to understand each other.

DORA: You know the village policeman was just here?

DEWI: I watched him come and go. He still has the same bike. I recognized its sound.

DORA: Did you hear what he said?

DEWI: Not a word. That's the worst of an old farmhouse like this. The walls and the floors are too thick for anyone upstairs even to hear shouting. . . That's why I came down . . . Was he . . . interesting?

JOHN: How did you come here, Dewi?

DEWI: Now, Dad, that's not honest. I'll bet you heard from the policeman, and you go inviting me to make up lies. I never tell lies unless they're convenient, to spare trouble for me or pain for the questioner. I'm much more normal than you suppose. I tell lies in just the same way as nice people.

DORA: You didn't come home in a lorry.

DEWI: No, of course not, or I wouldn't have been here for two more hours. Don't you remember I was fifth at Monte Carlo in my second year at college? But, Mam, the tale about the lorry spared you from suffering about that poor traveller for at least half an hour. I can't understand why you're not more grateful . . . How is he, by the way? . . . Did you hear?

JOHN: He's alive.

DEWI: Alive? Is he in danger?

JOHN: Not according to the report we had.

DEWI: Good. Murder isn't on my programme. I leave that to Providence.

JOHN: It would be a great help to me if I were allowed to know what *is* on your programme.

DEWI: You have a right to know that, Dad . . . First, staying here quietly for a night or two or three.

DORA: That's impossible, Dewi.

DEWI: Why?

DORA: Does it need to be said?

DEWI: You think the police will discover that little car? . . . Of course, they're bound to find it sometime or other. But not very quickly.

DORA: Where did you put the car?

DEWI: Mam, Mam! There's a question! All I'll say, just between you and me, is that — whatever the Free Wales Army may think — I'm very grateful to the Corporation of Liverpool for flooding a certain valley.

DORA: I see you enjoyed your supper.

DEWI: That apple tart was a treat after three months of cocoa and grease.

DORA: It's good that someone in this house is cheerful.

DEWI: Why not? I'm home. Everything's here but the fatted calf.

DORA: Really?

JOHN: My boy, is going back to prison for four or five years on your programme?

DEWI: Four years?

JOHN: For attacking a man and injuring him seriously and stealing his car and his money.

DEWI: I had no choice.

JOHN: Will you say that to the judge in court? . . . Because you'll be on *his* programme.

DEWI: You think so?

JOHN: Unfortunately, I'm sure of it.

DEWI: Seeing him once more sitting like a golliwog on his throne and giving me a sermon and four years? No. I've had that experience.

JOHN: Without learning anything?

DEWI: Dad, I chose that experience. It wasn't an accident. There was a thrill in the experience, and I wanted the thrill. I'm not sorry. I don't repent. But once is enough.

JOHN: Do you see a way to avoid repeating the experience?
(Dewi lights another cigarette and draws deep on the smoke before answering.)

DEWI: Listen, Dad, I came too quickly for the police to dream that I'm here. They won't discover the car for a pretty fair spell. If I manage to stay here quietly for three or four days, then they'll think I've turned south, in the direction of Cardiff or

138

Barry. Then it will be safe for me to make my way to Liverpool and cross over to Ireland . . . And that's the end of your worry. I'll go to America and you can forget about me.

DORA: Forget!

JOHN: *(downheartedly)* Dewi, it's very hard to believe that you graduated with honours.

DEWI: Long ago, Dad.

JOHN: You're talking like a child who hasn't grown up, dreaming dreams about trips to the moon. The police of Liverpool and Cardiff and Holyhead and Fishguard will be watching and searching for you, not for three days but for three months and a year. Your picture will be on every television screen in the realm tonight.

DEWI: *(quickly depressed)* It probably will.

JOHN: Listen. As a criminal you're an amateur, a boy on his own caught breaking into houses. To this very day I don't know why. But after being in prison you should know that the only successful criminals are those who belong to a professional gang, with money and resources in back of them. You're done for in crime if you play it solo.

DEWI: *(smiling)* Dad, I was expecting a sermon on morals. You talk just like my partner, a boxer from Stepney. He offered me a place in a gang after I complete my stretch. It was his opinion too that there wasn't much of a future for private enterprise.

JOHN: I'm glad to have the support of an expert. Tell him I value his opinion.

DEWI: Unfortunately, I won't see him tonight.

JOHN: Remember this, Dewi: if you want to join a gang, the earlier you start the better. A gangster is like a rugby player, he's at his best for some ten years at most.

DEWI: *(enjoying this)* Pretty good, minister! And so?

JOHN: And so, the right policy for you now is to make friends of the police. To call them on the telephone and wait courageously for them here. To let them know how to find the car and give them every help. And then they'll be likely to get the judge to reduce your sentence by a year or two. And remember that a gangster who is in partnership with the police is a pretty valuable member of the gang.

DEWI: Dad, may I thank you right now for not scolding and shouting threats and bellowing in my ears, and for not phoning the inspector in spite of me.

JOHN: I want you to do that yourself.

DEWI: I know . . . You think your love can save me.

JOHN: *(having received a terrible blow)* Well! . . . What about it?

DEWI: And I have come to the conclusion that love is a pleasant, transitory experience; but that I'm living in a world where love is completely meaningless, except as a biological factor, a convenient thing to carry on the race.

DORA: Dewi, I'll tell you this: if the police don't have a report about you within three days, they will come here with a warrant to search the house. Then your last chance to lessen your punishment will be gone.

DEWI: *(slowly and determinedly)* I am not going back to prison.

JOHN: *(trying to lighten the tension)* As far as that's concerned, nobody *goes* to prison. We'll be carried there, more than likely, all three of us.

DEWI: *(pressing his cigarette in the ash tray)* Dad, it was really pouring there one morning about a week ago. So, instead of going out to the yard for exercise, we had to walk around the narrow gallery on each floor in front of the cells. There are nets hanging across the hall under each gallery to catch anyone who tries to die by throwing himself off. There was one lad who stayed in his cell and refused to march. He stood in the corner of his cell with two night pots, one in each hand, defying the guards. He'd obviously lost his mind . . . Well, the guards have their methods. Two of the young ones came forwards, each with a heavy stick in the one hand, both of them holding a heavy mattress in front of them. They rush at the lad and bury him under the mattress. Within ten minutes he was covered with welts and left in the lunatics' cell. There isn't a scrap of bedclothes or furnishings of any sort in that cell . . . A week later he was back among us very quietly. Someone asked him what they did to him in solitary. He didn't answer. The dinner hour came. After three months we get dinner at tables on the floor of the hall. And he sat next to me yesterday. When the plates came and were passed around, he took a razor blade out of his pocket and struck

140

his brows and his eyes until they jumped onto the plates, a piece of his eyes on my plate, and blood was spurting onto the table. He was taken to hospital. No one ate dinner. This morning I ran away in the mist . . . and came home . . .

(Complete silence for a moment)

Mam, there was a Bible that used to be here all the time . . . Where is it?

(Dora gets the Bible and hands it to him)

. . . Here it is, the book of the covenant . . . This is what they swear to their lies on in the law court . . . All right, with this Bible in my hand I swear . . . that I will . . . not . . . go back to prison . . . come what may . . .

(He breaks down sobbing, as uncontrolled and shameless as a child . . . His parents look at him and then Dora goes to him to comfort him as the curtain falls.)

CURTAIN

ACT II

The same evening, about 10.15.
Dewi enters through the door on the left with Bet.

DEWI: You had no trouble coming?

BET: No trouble at all.

DEWI: Across the fields?

BET: I came along the main road through the village and then along this lane.

DEWI: You didn't see any police?

BET: The police are sure to be watching the fields for you. The village and the lane were clear. Besides, the vicar's daughter can call to see the minister's wife at ten o'clock, I suppose.

DEWI: Give me your coat.
(And she takes off her coat and the kerchief around her head and shakes her hair free. She is a beautiful girl, about twenty years old. Dewi puts her things on a chair.)

BET: Your story was on the news tonight on television.

DEWI: What did they say?

BET: That you cleared out in the mist and knocked some traveller on the head and took his car.

DEWI: And then?

BET: They gave the number of the car and asked for any information.

DEWI: Do you despise me?

BET: You did phone me.

DEWI: I took a chance.

BET: And here I am.

DEWI: My life is in your hands.

BET: Very well. Give me a kiss.
        (They embrace and kiss)
        . . . Oh Dewi!
DEWI: Cigarette?
BET: Thanks.
        (He strikes a light and both smoke.)
DEWI: I haven't anything to drink here. A minister's house.
BET: I haven't anything to drink over there. The vicar's house.
        (They both laugh . . . pause)
DEWI: Well?
BET: I don't know how to begin, Dewi.
DEWI: Neither do I.
BET: Seeing you is . . . like waking up from a nightmare. Yes, a
        nightmare.
DEWI: Were you worried?
BET: Don't begin that way.
DEWI: The best thing is to start as people do at a social. Isn't it an
        awful night? Did you get wet in coming?
BET: No, thank you, sir. There wasn't any rain. I didn't get wet.
DEWI: And how is the vicar these days? Is he in good health?
BET: A bit of a convenient cough. He's just gone to bed. Most of
        the time he goes to his perch at about eleven.
DEWI: You're still keeping house for him?
BET: I have no choice now that Gran's dead.
DEWI: You won't go back to college?
BET: I could hardly leave him. I don't know. I'd like to go back
        . . . And you?
DEWI: What?
BET: Will you go back to the college?
DEWI: Hardly.
BET: There would be a thrill in going back.
DEWI: Thrill?
BET: Or excitement. Those were always your great words. From
        excitement to excitement or from thrill to thrill, that was
        living . . . I never thought you took it so seriously.
DEWI: Philosophy, you see. After Marx philosophy isn't under-
        standing the world — it's changing the world.
BET: And you've changed your life.

DEWI:	There's no going back. I left another college this morning, after finishing only three months of the course.
BET:	The course wasn't to your liking?
DEWI:	Sewing postal bags morning, noon, and night. I learned a lot about the crisis of absurdity.
BET:	That's why . . .?
DEWI:	That's why there's no going back.
BET:	I'm afraid to ask my next question . . .
DEWI:	Of course. What are you giving the vicar for his cough?
BET:	If I had arsenic, I'd give you a cupful this minute.
DEWI:	Don't talk flippantly of serious things. That would be the best thing for me.
BET:	Don't you talk seriously about facetious things. Three quarters of our love was fun and laughter. "Long may the old language endure."
DEWI:	Even after three months of prison!
BET:	Has it killed your sense of humour?
DEWI:	Hard to say. In prison all laughter is partly malice. The ones who aren't all there, they're the only ones who laugh happily.
BET:	Don't be heartbroken. That's true of the church and the chapel and the women's hostel at college. People who are also in prison.
DEWI:	Where there are people there's hell.
BET:	And sometimes, for half an hour, when there are only two, a glimpse of heaven.
DEWI:	Do you think there's a chance I can escape to America?
BET:	That's your heaven?
DEWI:	It isn't as confined there as in prison. More room.
BET:	When do you intend to start?
DEWI:	This next month.
BET:	How much money do you have?
DEWI:	*(taking money out of his pocket)* Three shillings and a groat.
BET:	Where did you get that much?
DEWI:	The remains of the traveller's money.
BET:	Poor thing.
DEWI:	Me or the traveller?
BET:	Both, I suppose.
DEWI:	I'd give a great deal to be in his place.
BET:	Thank you, sir, for the compliment.

DEWI: That's why I was thinking of going to America.

BET: You used to be more original than that. Everyone who's on the run from the law wants to go to America.

DEWI: Everyone? The voice of the majority is the voice of God. Everyone in Wales believes that.

BET: And everyone in prison?

DEWI: We're odd ones in prison. The body's as greedy as death, although they put dope in the cocoa to keep a man's spirit low and tame. But no one in prison thinks that being there is part of his life. It's an interval between living and living. Everyone plans to start living again after he's finished his spell there. Even the ones who are there for life.

BET: You too?

DEWI: Without that who would escape?

BET: But it was an experience?

DEWI: "The more a man lives, The more he sees and hears."

BET: You didn't find any excitement there, any thrill?

DEWI: The best thrill I had was driving away in the mist this morning.

BET: Like Monte Carlo?

DEWI: Better than Monte Carlo. I've never driven better. I was across the Gloucester bridge, the only spot where there was a risk the police would be waiting for me, before the mist rose. After that the road was clear and I was singing . . . Singing, you know!

BET: Was the countryside terrified?
(*The telephone rings*)

DEWI: Always the police again!

BET: Shall I answer? . . .
(*She picks up the telephone and makes her voice older*)
. . . Tan-y-fron two-three-seven . . . Mrs Rhys here . . . What? What? . . . I'm sorry, I don't understand what you're saying . . . English? Not a word . . . Oh, you can speak Welsh? . . . There you are, lad, what do you want . . . A reporter! . . . What is a reporter? . . . The *Mercury* . . . ? I've never heard of the *Mercury* . . . A daily paper? . . . Good heavens, are there people who see a newspaper every day? . . . I get the news in the *Goleuad*, you see . . . Yes, yes, living in the country, a minister's wife . . . What did you say? . . .

Have the police been here? Yes, to be sure, hundreds of them all day like crows nesting . . . Yes, looking for my son, they said . . . Have I any idea where he is? . . . We had a telegram from him, you see . . . Did we show the telegram to the police? No danger of that, it was a private telegram to his mother . . . What was in the telegram? . . . Well, you understand, just the name of that girl . . . What girl? The girl he ran off to meet . . . Yes, it was to meet the girl that he ran away . . . Can you put the girl's name in the paper? . . . Yes, I suppose . . . Let me look for her name in the telegram . . . Yes, here it is, Goto Hell [*she pronounces this with Welsh vowel-sounds and "ll"*] . . . rather like the *Tŷ Hyll* on the road to Capel Gurig, you know . . . What? . . . I'll spell it for you . . . Gee-oh-tee-oh, Aitch-ee-el-el. . . A definite scoop for you . . . Good night, reporter . . .
(She puts the telephone in its cradle and Dewi takes her in his arms and they dance humming the tune . . . Then –)

DEWI: Thank you, Bet . . . There are still some moments, some moments . . .

BET: Dewi, it's almost six months . . .

DEWI: I know, I know.

BET: The first I heard was whispers at supper table in the hostel. None of the girls was ready to speak plainly. "Have you heard anything of Dewi Rhys?", that was all, and they'd turn away.

DEWI: I hate women. A man has no weapons against them.

BET: The next morning I saw the story of your arrest in the paper.

DEWI: I couldn't ask the inspector to invite you to the station.

BET: From then until tonight, until the telephone tonight, not one word . . . An iron curtain . . . After three months of being out with each other part of every day.

DEWI: Can't you see that that's why?

BET: But you phoned tonight.

DEWI: It was dangerous . . . But I couldn't not phone . . . You came.

BET: Do you . . .

DEWI: What?

BET: Do you despise me . . . for coming?

146

DEWI: Despise you!
        (He starts towards her, but she raises her hand to stop him)
BET: No. Don't. We need to talk seriously, not play games.
DEWI: Play games, Bet!
BET: You didn't come home to see me.
DEWI: I *wanted* to see you.
BET: Probably. But that was something you thought of after you arrived. There was a thrill in the shock of it.
DEWI: Love *is* a thrill. You can't deny it.
BET: I suppose pretending to love is also a thrill?
DEWI: I know. I've hurt you.
BET: I was glad for an excuse to leave the hostel and the college. Yes, you did hurt me. I confess it. No one else could hurt me.
DEWI: That's some comfort.
BET: You're hateful.
DEWI: Yes . . . Why?
BET: Because you're so sure of me.
DEWI: And you?
BET: No. I'm not at all sure of you.
DEWI: What's shaken your faith?
BET: Need you ask?
DEWI: Prison? Because I'm a thief? I've broken into shops? I've destroyed my career, my good name? I've brought shame on you at the college? Because there's no chance now for us ever to be married? The vicar's daughter in love with a convict!
BET: Keep going, Dewi! You know that not one of your arrows has touched me.
DEWI: They should, you know. Those arrows have a bit of a point to them. After all, you're one of the Welsh *bourgeoisie.*
BET: And you?
DEWI: So was I until six months ago . . . Not now. I've been excommunicated!
BET: Do you think that shocks me?
DEWI: All right, what do you have against me?
BET: I'm ashamed to say.
DEWI: We're to talk seriously, you said, not play games.
BET: What I have against you is that I've lost my heart to you, I've loved you, *love* you . . . and I don't know at this very moment whether that counts for anything at all in your life.

147

DEWI: Because I didn't write? Because I refused to see you before the trial? And you were there, in the gallery, the second seat from the door. I stood up right away after the judge pronounced the sentence. And I didn't look at you or give any sign that I saw you.

BET: Shut up, Dewi, shut up!

DEWI: What else?

BET: The case against you named five dates, five nights when you broke into a shop or a garage and stole. On three of those evenings we were together from six o'clock until closing time for the hostel. Then you left me and started off on your motor-bike . . .

DEWI: *(smiling)* Did you want to come with me?

BET: That would have been better than being deceived like a child.

DEWI: I never deceived you, girl, never. I can almost say that you're the only one, the only one, that I've never intentionally deceived. Damn you!

BET: Don't say the things I'm longing to hear . . . I can't bear it . . . *(She blows her nose and dries her eyes and then turns angrily on him)* . . . I hate blowing my nose. If it weren't for you I wouldn't have to.

DEWI: If there were no "ifs" or "werent's" . . . Do you still go to church?

BET: I play the harmonium there.

DEWI: For your father's sake?

BET: Partly, perhaps.

DEWI: And on holidays from the college I used to go to chapel for Dad's and Mam's sake, so as not to hurt them. That's wrong. That's where deception begins.

BET: I think I'd go to church apart from Daddy.

DEWI: Can you believe in that stuff?

BET: I can't help it. It's in my blood.

DEWI: That was your argument long ago. You haven't changed?

BET: And you would argue ferociously that God is dead.

DEWI: And then go straight off to break into a garage. Definite proof that morality without religion is impossible. Therefore God exists and prison is a blessing.

BET: I never said anything of the kind. I wasn't blaming you. I never had a course in philosophy.

DEWI: That's blaming me now.

BET: The only thing I blamed you for was excluding me from your secret and your life.

DEWI: Tell that to your father. The vicar will answer that that's the only honourable thing he's heard of me in his whole life.

BET: What was it all about, Dewi? A joke?

DEWI: Another cigarette?

BET: No.

(Dewi lights up, then walks and comes back to her)

DEWI: It was a joke while it lasted. I'd sit a sociology exam in the morning, and do a job in a supermarket the same night. A pleasant contrast, and yet I saw the connection between them.

BET: What else? The excitement? The thrill?

DEWI: Good Lord! Like climbing an impossible slope and clawing for a place to hold on. Every nerve in my body was like a harpstring. I'd sleep a whole day in bed after finishing a job, sleep like a child, my nerves completely done in . . . I've always been like that, living on my nerves, and sometimes they'd break down entirely and leave me crying like a child . . . Only sometimes.

BET: What drove you to it? It wasn't the money. They found almost all the money in your desk.

DEWI: I was a fool about the money. I'm ashamed of that at this very moment. Honesty about money is made the standard of bourgeois morality in Wales. You hear it at a funeral, "He paid his way honestly. He didn't leave any debts." Honest! There's a sound of servile slavery in the word! The slavery of the little Welsh students at the college who look forwards without hate or fear to forty years of being schoolteachers, with a little pension as a star before them to the end of the journey. Slavery!

BET: So rebellion was the starting point? Rebellion against the fear and the lack of daring of Wales?

DEWI: That helped.

BET: Helped? That wasn't the start?

DEWI: That wasn't the start.

BET: Dewi, I have a right to know what made you start.

DEWI: Yes, I suppose so.

BET: Well?

DEWI: You.

BET: Me? . . . Impossible.

DEWI: Do you remember the meeting at Dolgellau post-office, — when you and your friends sat down in the office to protest against the contempt for the Welsh language there?

BET: I remember that day very well.

DEWI: You'd said that you wanted to go with the march.

BET: And you were fiercely against it and insisted that every campaign of that sort in Wales faded out. That they weren't serious.

DEWI: I followed you to see.

BET: What did you see?

DEWI: I saw the police carry you and the others out of the office and throw you down on the square. I saw the scum of Dolgellau kick you and pull you by the hair and treat the others the same way. I saw the police let them do it and the crowd stand idle, as I did, without moving a finger to protect you.

BET: I wasn't much hurt, Dewi.

DEWI: Maybe not. I'd gone there to see if Wales could give me excitement in life. I left there in a fury, cursing the whole world, and Wales. And the following Sunday night I broke into a garage and stole twenty pounds.

BET: To avenge us?

DEWI: No, not to avenge anyone. But to cut myself off forever from people so insipid that they have no respect for their country or their language, because they have no respect for themselves.

BET: And so you too are a nationalist?

DEWI: A lot of nonsense! I can't be a nationalist where the nation is dead, long dead.

BET: I am *Welsh*.

DEWI: I know. It stinks.

BET: I thought your kiss was rather brief.

DEWI: You're devoting yourself to things that are dead or about to die. God, religion, church or chapel, Wales, the Welsh

150

	language, — that's your world. Believe you me, Capel Celyn under water is a parable of Wales and all her chapels.
BET:	I can't deny that that's the danger. To me, too, it was the cowardice of Wales, not the Corporation of Liverpool, that betrayed Capel Celyn. But then . . . what is your choice?
DEWI:	What is left for a man without a nation, with nothing to believe in, with nothing to be faithful to —
BET:	Nothing to be faithful to?
DEWI:	There's only one thing left besides Communism, — himself. I can't turn communist. Wales has had her bellyful of Puritanism. The Communist way of life is Puritanism without God. With nuclear war waiting to destroy its whole foundation. No, I must create my own meaning in life. I must choose, and in choosing stand alone facing the world and society, turn life into a challenge and a thrill. Defy society, defy law and opinion, choose the life of a criminal and an outlaw. That's the answer to the crisis of absurdity. Hitler had a country and a nation to play with and give him excitement in living, and then he died of his own will. I have nothing, nothing but my own life. *I* am Tomorrow's Wales!
BET:	Sh! . . . A motor-bike in the lane . . . At this time of night!
DEWI:	Jones the policeman.
BET:	He's not passing . . . He's coming here . . . He's here!
	(A heavy knock at the door of the house)
DEWI:	Dad will let him in . . . There he is on the stairs.
BET:	Get into the kitchen, quickly . . . I'll stay here.
	(Dewi exits, left. Bet lights a cigarette and stands self-possessed by the fire facing the room. The centre door opens. John Rhys's voice, "Come in." Jones enters with his helmet under his arm, and nods at Bet. She bows her head an inch. John comes behind the policeman, sees Bet, has a shock of great fright, controls himself before the policeman sees anything.)
BET:	Mrs Rhys has gone upstairs, Mr Rhys.
JOHN:	Have you news for me, Constable?
BET:	Am I in the way, Mr Rhys?
JOHN:	No, please stay, Miss Edward. The constable has nothing to say that you can't hear. He's a familiar visitor by now.
JONES:	Quite unofficially this time, sir. I saw the light in your study and I thought of you there, suffering and worrying, and you

151

a minister here too. Then I thought there wouldn't be any harm in giving you a word of news.

JOHN: That's kind of you. Is there any comfort in the news?

JONES: I hope so. At first the police had a bit of a fright. Then, after a search, they gathered that nothing unfortunate had happened.

JOHN: Nothing unfortunate?

JONES: The police have found the traveller's car.

JOHN: You don't say! . . . Pretty good, indeed. Quick too . . . Undamaged?

JONES: I don't know for sure. More than likely.

JOHN: Where was it found?

JONES: Well, there it is, sir. I don't have permission to say where. We were warned not to say until tomorrow. But there's no harm in my telling you this much privately: less than ten miles from here.

JOHN: Well, well!

JONES: It's fairly certain that the driver wasn't injured.

JOHN: He was on his way home then. That is some comfort.

JONES: More than likely. Of course, we can't be sure. There could be something else that's attracting him. But the inspector expects to find him around here in the dark tonight . . . You don't have any relatives in these parts, Mr Rhys?

JOHN: No one this side of the Menai.

JONES: Or Mrs Rhys either?

JOHN: No one within ten miles.

JONES: There it is. Sometimes there are others besides relatives . . . If we discover him, I've no doubt that you will hear very quickly. In my opinion your worry will be over very soon.

JOHN: What will the procedure be then?

JONES: He'll be taken to town first. It's possible you'll get permission to see him there.

JOHN: In rather sad circumstances.

JONES: I thought you would sleep better, perhaps, if you heard this much.

JOHN: You're very kind. Having a constable in the village who's a neighbour is a comfort . . . Is there any further news about the traveller?

JONES:	Fairly comforting. He'll be mended enough, quite certainly, to testify at the trial.
JOHN:	Of course! There'll be another trial.
JONES:	If I may offer a suggestion, Mr Rhys . . .
JOHN:	I'll be grateful for any help.
JONES:	Having a psychiatrist examine him would be the best chance for the defence. I heard of a poet-preacher some time ago. There was something strange in that too. But God help us, a philosopher-thief! That can't be normal.
JOHN:	It can't, can it? But which of us is normal in this country today?
JONES:	*(turning to go)* May I ask, Miss Edward, how the vicar is?
BET:	He's had a touch of a cold, Mr Jones.
JONES:	Mrs Roberts, who works for you, said that she heard you phoning for the doctor tonight. She lives next door to me. She thought you'd had a bit of a fright.
BET:	Well, yes, a bit . . . Good night.
	(Exit Jones and John. Bet puts out her cigarette irritably. John returns)
JOHN:	Bet!
BET:	I'm terribly sorry, Mr Rhys.
JOHN:	I was that close to giving him away.
BET:	You have better nerves than your son. A hundred times better than mine.
JOHN:	It was just luck that I was behind the policeman.
BET:	I had to stay here. The policeman knew that you were in the study.
JOHN:	I never draw the curtains on the study windows.
BET:	It was natural for me to be smoking here and to be company for Mrs Rhys. You didn't tell a lie.
JOHN:	When did you come?
BET:	About ten o'clock.
JOHN:	You knew about him?
BET:	Dewi phoned from here. I had phoned the doctor a minute earlier. Or Mrs Roberts would have answered the phone.
JOHN:	Does your father know?
BET:	That I came here?
JOHN:	To Dewi?
BET:	No. He went to bed early because of his cold.

JOHN: Then he hasn't heard the report?

BET: He didn't watch television or hear the news.

JOHN: I'm putting your father in jeopardy.

BET: You? How, Mr Rhys?

JOHN: Each of us here tonight is breaking the law, hiding a criminal who has been sentenced to prison . . . From the standpoint of the law it's a rather serious offence.

BET: That never entered my mind.

JOHN: Your father and I are friends. He was kind beyond anything that was called for when the story about Dewi first came out. And now here I am bringing trouble on him.

BET: I'm beginning to understand Dewi. There's a thrill, there really is, in breaking the law.

JOHN: Your father is the vicar of the parish.

BET: And you're a minister, Mr Rhys. It's hard on religion in Wales!

JOHN: Being his father prevents me from seeing the funny side of the situation.

BET: Forgive me, Mr Rhys. You're right. It isn't funny. And I don't see it as funny either. Just the opposite. But joking for a moment helps . . . to keep from crying.

JOHN: The police are closing in around us.

BET: Do you think the only purpose of the constable just now was to do you a favour?

JOHN: He too must seize every chance that presents itself.

BET: He asked a few questions too.

JOHN: Things are close to coming to a head for the boy. By tomorrow they'll know that he's here.

BET: Give him tonight, Mr Rhys. Let him have tonight.

JOHN: We've had to consider that, and more. His mother and I. Now you're here too and the police have found you here. I'm bringing you and your father into my family's trouble.

BET: I've been in the trouble from the start.

JOHN: You, Bet? . . . *(No answer)* . . . I suspected that the police-man knew something I didn't know . . . Bet, are you and Dewi . . . more than friends? I've never asked Dewi . . . I have a right to know now.

BET: *(low, intense, but without crying)* That's why I'm here . . . He called . . . What will I do, Mr Rhys? What will I do? . . . If he called from Hell, I would go.

JOHN: What about *him*?

BET: I don't know.

JOHN: Does he —

BET: Don't ask that, Mr Rhys. That's the question I don't dare ask myself.

JOHN: This changes everything, Bet . . . Changes everything.
(Dewi enters from the left)

DEWI: At last! I slipped out through the back and watched him from the garden. He sat on his bike a long time looking over the house . . . Is there a light in the attic room, Dad? He was staring up there hard, as though he expected to see me on top of the roof.

JOHN: There are dust and books and old furniture there. There's no light.

DEWI: I know. I used to play hide-and-seek there with Mam long ago. It's a fine place to hide.

JOHN: For a child. Not for a full-grown man.

DEWI: Do they suspect, I wonder, that I'm here?

JOHN: Yes.

DEWI: You're as encouraging as Job's comforters.

JOHN: The policeman offered comfort.

DEWI: Did he? He brought the news that I'd drowned?

JOHN: Hardly, when he was searching the rooftop for you.

DEWI: Logic! He had news then?

JOHN: They've found the traveller's car.

DEWI: No!

JOHN: Yes.

DEWI: And he came here to tell you that?

JOHN: That's what he said.

DEWI: I've never liked the man.

JOHN: It's all up with you for escaping from here now.

DEWI: *(taking money from his pocket)* Dad, I'll bet three shillings and a groat against ten shillings that I still have a chance.

JOHN: You're in very high spritis.

DEWI: Seeing a policeman turn his back on me gives my heart a lift like dinner-time.

JOHN: I saw you behave very differently two hours ago.

DEWI: I'm a fickle person, Dad, fickle, fickle. Not like Bet.

JOHN: Dewi, there's a coarseness in your speech that the company in prison does not excuse. Leave Bet alone.

DEWI: Leave her alone? . . . I would if I were godly . . . I'm not godly.

JOHN: Phoning her tonight was much more cruel than hitting the traveller with a crank.

BET: It's my fault, Mr Rhys, I wanted to come.

JOHN: You have no mercy.

DEWI: Mercy?

JOHN: None.

DEWI: Do you want mercy, Bet?

BET: I will, perhaps, tomorrow.

JOHN: Bet, I have an obligation to tell you now that you must put an end to this.

BET: *(slowly)* I know that, Mr Rhys, I know that.

JOHN: Are you going to do that now? Make a clean break?

BET: *(sadly and finally)* No.
(A gesture of despair from John)

JOHN: What is there left for me to do? . . . For your sake and your father's I must phone the police.

BET: You promised him tonight. This is not the way we should be talking to each other, Mr Rhys.

JOHN: And your father?

BET: Daddy knows. After the trial I poured it all out to him.

JOHN: What did he say?

BET: He didn't say much . . . He's a vicar, not a preacher.

JOHN: It would be better if you went home now.

BET: Yes, probably . . . May I stay a little while, Mr Rhys? Six months ago . . . at college . . . before there was a hint of trouble, — there hasn't been a word between us since then.

JOHN: I'll leave you. Bless you, my girl . . . If you can persuade this boy to call the police himself tomorrow morning, it can lighten his sentence a bit.
(Exit John . . . Dewi begins to laugh)

BET: Not one word now about your father.

DEWI: Very well, my lady . . . What shall we talk about?

BET: About the future, of course.

DEWI: Is there a future?

BET: We won't have an opportunity after tonight.

DEWI: So you think there's a chance for me to escape to America?

BET: About the future I said. Not about novels.

DEWI: Without imagination there is no future.

BET: That's philosophy. I know that the sun will rise tomorrow and the police will come here to search the house, imagination or not.

DEWI: There's not much excitement in your future. I see it as rather flat.

BET: I'm a woman.

DEWI: You know, I've suspected that for some time.

BET: A woman doesn't only imagine the future — she shapes the future, carries the future, nurses the future. That's what her womb is good for.

DEWI: *(ironic)* Miss Edward, there's a sound like wedding bells in your words . . . You haven't made plans to marry?

BET: Yes, Dewi . . . Does it matter to you?

DEWI: *(somewhat nonplussed)* Well, after our talk tonight, I must confess that the news is rather odd.

BET: I'm sorry. But all the talk was about you. I didn't have much of a chance to say a great deal about myself.

DEWI: May I be so bold as to ask, who is the unfortunate young man?

BET: I knew him at college.

DEWI: Do I know him?

BET: I don't know . . . I have my doubts.

DEWI: Well, who is the devil?

BET: You.

DEWI: *(after a space of smiling and walking)* You won that one.

BET: No, the game isn't over.

DEWI: The vicar's daughter . . . ?

BET: The son of the manse . . . An ecumenical union.

DEWI: Marrying a thief, a fugitive from jail, a convict.

BET: Don't be so conventional, so bourgois, so Welsh!

DEWI: Conventional? You're the one talking about getting married.

BET: To a girl there's excitement in getting married. And a sacrament is not a convention.

157

DEWI:	Don't tempt me, Bet. I've been fairly honourable with you.
BET:	If it's tempting you to save you, to win you, I'm not ashamed of tempting you.
DEWI:	You don't know. I'm a filthy pig.
BET:	I love you and you know that, you pig.
DEWI:	It's impossible now.
BET:	America is impossible. The romance of the outlaw life is impossible. But love can defy convention and society, yes, and defy suffering.
DEWI:	You're asking me to go back to prison in handcuffs?
BET:	Do you dare? Do you have enough guts?
DEWI:	You haven't the least notion what you're asking.
BET:	I haven't any idea. But, Dewi, have you looked at your mother's hair? Six months ago it was the same colour as yours . . . And you can't comprehend the secret of that change.
DEWI:	You know that you're turning the whole principle of my life upside down? Every oath I swore to myself?
BET:	You did the phoning. Not me.
DEWI:	I'd resolved to cast love out of my life.
BET:	Do that. But take me into it.
DEWI:	Are you in your right mind?
BET:	It's hard for me. I've had to throw away all womanly modesty. Because we have only tonight.
DEWI:	We have only tonight. Tonight is our fate.
BET:	I want children, Dewi, your children. I want that thrill, to sing my Gran's lullabies to your sons. You see, if there's no Welsh nation for you to be faithful to, I want to make one; and love it too.
DEWI:	You're snatching me too into your foolish dream.
BET:	Will you phone the inspector tomorrow?
DEWI:	I must have proof, Bet.
BET:	Proof of what?
DEWI:	That you'll be waiting for me if I come out. There won't be a second escape.
BET:	Of the pair of us, I'm not the one who's fickle.
DEWI:	You're asking me to choose two years or more of prison, reach out my hands willingly for the cuffs, bow my head, go back.

BET: Go back because that way there's the door of hope.

DEWI: You've never seen a prison door from the inside.

BET: I'll be there when the morning comes to open it.

DEWI: A promise to keep me from going mad?

BET: Myself, body and soul, to keep you.

DEWI: On your oath?

BET: On my word, which is enough, if you'll go back.

DEWI: Tonight is the proof of that.

BET: Proof?

DEWI: How can I go back without having proof?

BET: What proof can I give?

DEWI: I need to carry the memory of it like a lamp in my bosom through the darkness of the years in the clink.

BET: Speak your mind plainly.

DEWI: Stay with me tonight. All night tonight in my arms. I won't go back without that.

BET: I'm an old-fashioned girl, Dewi. I've always thought of it as coming through the door of the sacrament.

DEWI: I have only tonight, Bet. You understand, I have only tonight. Tonight is our sacrament.

BET: *(slowly, in pain)* If I stay tonight?

DEWI: You can phone the inspector in the morning.

BET: *(reaching her hands to him without a smile)* A husband's promise . . . ?

DEWI: *(taking her hands without a kiss or a smile)* To his wife.

CURTAIN

ACT III

Next day, 7 a.m.
John in an old coat, with a beret on his head and work gloves on his hands, is finishing laying a fire and cleaning the hearth. Dora comes from the kitchen and looks through the window. She is dressed for early morning in a beautiful housecoat.

DORA: It isn't raining.

JOHN: A pretty fair morning.

DORA: You've pulled the curtains back.

JOHN: No one's died here up to now . . . That's strange too.

DORA: He'll have to stay upstairs then.

JOHN: Oh? . . . I didn't think of that . . . Yes, while he's here.

DORA: There's nothing else to do. The police would notice and call if the curtains were across the windows all day.

JOHN: He can sit in the study. It's safe there as long as he doesn't stand in the window.

DORA: We're more afraid of the day than the night.

JOHN: Evil-doers.

DORA: Drawing the curtains and locking the doors at night is a refuge.

JOHN: I doubt that he'll have a second night here.

DORA: I haven't thought about tonight. Today is ahead of us. This morning.

JOHN: The day's become a nightmare.

DORA: I can't believe that I'm preparing breakfast for three, and he's lurking there, like a fox with the hounds on his trail. Tell me, is it really true?

JOHN: Ask Dewi. He's the philosopher.

160

DORA: He doesn't believe truth exists.

JOHN: I envy him.

DORA: You?

JOHN: He's normal. Eight out of ten people in Wales think as he does, that there is no truth.

DORA: That's why he's searching for something to put excitement in his life?

JOHN: Other people find it on the television set, in English pop songs from Liverpool.

DORA: An escape from life?

JOHN: A failure to live. An escape from the failure, from the endless daily boredom. One has to be very frivolous to enjoy one's daily bread.

DORA: Are you offering me comfort? Showing that Dewi's life is not all bad?

JOHN: He terrifies me. Because I can't condemn him. I have only pity for him, and that there's no way to save him.

DORA: And you didn't sleep all night last night.

JOHN: Who could sleep? Did you hear the policeman?

DORA: And you going downstairs to let him in. It was almost eleven o'clock.

JOHN: Were you frightened?

DORA: It's a strange thing — knowing that he was sleeping there, his own dear self, under the same roof, the policeman's knock didn't disturb me as much.

JOHN: I told him to come in, and I opened this parlour door, without considering for a moment that there was a risk.

DORA: A risk?

JOHN: Dewi was here in the parlour half a minute earlier.

DORA: That wasn't a risk — it was an opportunity.

JOHN: No, no. He'd be like a mouse in a trap.

DORA: But safe.

JOHN: I can't save him by a trick.

DORA: Really?

JOHN: What are you thinking?

DORA: There's not a single trick that wouldn't be fair to save him . . . But don't make a mistake with anyone else.

JOHN: Bet isn't a trick to save him.

DORA: You left her here with him.

161

JOHN: Yes, after the policeman had gone.

DORA: Was that fair to Bet?

JOHN: She begged me to.

DORA: Of course. And you agreed.

JOHN: What else could I do?

DORA: That wasn't a trick?

JOHN: What sort of trick?

DORA: A trick to have her do what we have an obligation to do. To persuade him to give himself up to the police.

JOHN: I don't believe she could ever do that either.

DORA: And despite that, you begged her to try?

JOHN: Was that unfair?

DORA: It's impossible not to be unfair.

JOHN: I would hate to do wrong to Bet.

DORA: Everyone in the village knows that Dewi was going out with her at college.

JOHN: I didn't know, until last night.

DORA: You're a minister.

JOHN: And you didn't say anything.

DORA: I'm a woman, and a mother.

JOHN: The policeman acted as though he expected to find her here.

DORA: And find him here with her as well.

JOHN: It came very close to that.

DORA: It's certain that he has some suspicion of that too. The net is closing around us.

JOHN: They suspect that he's here but they don't have enough evidence. My opinion now is that they sent Jones here last night to frighten us so that we wouldn't give him shelter.

DORA: They're afraid of an uproar, too, from searching a minister's house without a good reason.

JOHN: I can't remain a minister after this.

DORA: Why not?

JOHN: Once a person interferes with the law, his sympathy naturally tends to side with the criminal.

DORA: This criminal is your son.

JOHN: He isn't to blame for that.

DORA: It's natural for us to try to hide him.

JOHN: If I knew of one way in the world to hide him safely, I'd do it now.

162

DORA: John, you're growing more like a Christian every day. Especially in those clothes.

JOHN: But there's no way. They'll come here with a warrant to search the house.

DORA: Is escape impossible?

JOHN: I sold the car to pay the lawyer last time.

DORA: It's a good thing we don't have a car.

JOHN: I don't know.

DORA: Where would he go?

JOHN: He could drive for his life.

DORA: Race? To where?

JOHN: Like Lawrence of Arabia.

DORA: . . . No, John, no.

JOHN: Eighty miles an hour on a winding road. There's a real thrill in ending like that.

DORA: Thank goodness we don't have a car.

JOHN: Do you see why I can't condemn him? If the boy is a thief and struck a man half-dead on the highway, I am his father and I can imagine his death. I'm a murderer myself. He awakens things in my unconscious that make me unable to look at him without guilt and fear.

DORA: No one is responsible for the things that flash suddenly into the mind. Or every married woman in that chapel would be a whore.

JOHN: It was as suddenly as that that Dewi struck the traveller. Like a lightning-bolt, all at once, came the opportunity and the idea. And then all the police in the realm are on his trail. And I, the murderer who could see him, a corpse in his car at the side of the road, enter the pulpit to preach.

DORA: A sleepless night, tossing and turning with worry, that's what you're guilty of.

JOHN: That's why, if there were any chance at all that he could escape, I'd do everything to help him now.

DORA: That oath on the Bible last night, and all that crying . . .

JOHN: He swore that he wouldn't go back.

DORA: Was it the truth or was he acting?

JOHN: Good acting *is* the truth, for the actor himself at the moment.

163

DORA: I don't know about that. But I do know that Dewi watches himself acting, and enjoys it.

JOHN: Without anything else to hold onto, to believe in, what else can he do? He has to turn his life into a show for himself. That's the damnation of the artist.

DORA: If he could only stop acting in time, before he destroys himself.

JOHN: There's nothing for it but to beg him once more to phone the Inspector himself this morning.

DORA: And then, if he refuses?

JOHN: He *will* refuse. And you know it.

DORA: Yes . . . And then?

JOHN: I don't know.

DORA: Will you do it?

JOHN: Phone?

DORA: Yes.

JOHN: The act would be over then. And I'd really be a murderer.

DORA: All right. I'll phone. I'm his mother. Love must also take risks.

JOHN: He's likely to sleep late. He used to sleep a long time after every examination. He lives on his nerves and wears himself out.

DORA: Go wash and shave. Breakfast will be ready soon. Then, we phone . . . me or him.

(Dora exits left and John after her. A short pause. Bet enters through the middle door, looks at the room, looks through the window, goes to the telephone and dials quickly, listens)

BET: Police Station? . . . Is Inspector Evans there? . . . No? Will you give him an urgent message? . . . Ready? . . . Dewi Rhys, who escaped from prison yesterday, is here at the manse, in his parents' house. He is willing to put himself in the hands of the police . . . He is waiting for you here . . . You needn't fear that he'll try to escape. This is his own choice and his own decision . . . Who's phoning? Say that it's his mother . . .

(She puts the telephone back in its cradle. Dora comes to the door left, frightened)

DORA: Bet!

BET: Yes, it's me, Mrs Rhys. Did I frighten you? I'm sorry.

DORA: I heard talking. Everything frightens me now, especially voices.

BET: I was phoning. Forgive me.

DORA: You're welcome here. But where did you come from so early? Who let you in?

BET: I slept here last night, Mrs Rhys.

DORA: Here? Bet, is your father —

BET: No, Daddy's all right . . . Dewi asked me.

DORA: Dewi?

BET: I slept with Dewi.

DORA: *(sitting down grief-stricken)* No! . . . No!
(Pause)

BET: He's sleeping now . . . sleeping like a child . . . without a worry or fear . . . Mrs Rhys?

DORA: Yes?
(A pause. Dora turns to look at her)

BET: Don't turn me out.

DORA: Come here, Bet.
(Bet kneels beside her; Dora kisses her tenderly)

BET: I may stay?

DORA: You don't remember your mother?

BET: I was four years old when she was buried. Gran brought me up.

DORA: And I never had a daughter, — until now.

BET: There was only Dewi?

DORA: I lost his brother.

BET: An only child is a risk.

DORA: Every child is a risk.

BET: Every love is a risk.

DORA: You do love him?

BET: Yes . . . hopelessly . . . Worse luck.

DORA: Without counting the cost.

BET: I give what I can.

DORA: You give too much, Bet, you give too much. Aren't you afraid?

BET: If I can give him hope, if I can give him love?

DORA: There's nothing for it then, no help at all . . . He will break your heart.

BET: Yes . . . I know.

DORA: And you gave yourself in spite of that?

BET: So that he'll go back.

DORA: To prison?

BET: This morning. The beginning of hope, the beginning of accepting life as it is. I must be here to see that. To see him laugh.

DORA: He insisted that you stay last night?

BET: Otherwise he refused to go back.

DORA: That was the price?

BET: That was the price. No, it wasn't a price. The kiss of life.

DORA: An unfair price.

BET: But I'm glad now. Whatever happens, I'm glad now.

DORA: Was that all?

BET: I've promised to marry him.

DORA: After he completes his sentence?

BET: The morning he comes out of prison.

DORA: On the condition that he phone the police today?

BET: On the condition that I could phone the inspector this morning in his name.

DORA: Was that absolutely clear?

BET: As a marriage vow.

DORA: Are you going to phone, Bet?

BET: I've just done it. They're probably on their way here now.

DORA: *(rising and raising Bet in fear)* What?

BET: That's what you heard from the kitchen just now. I phoned so that he could sleep until the moment came.

DORA: Bet, my dear, you must face the worst.

BET: He's ready now. He put his hands in mine.

DORA: That was last night.

BET: And I gave myself to him completely.

DORA: You've won my love as well. My love and my thanks. But I'm afraid for you.

BET: Have I won *his* love?

DORA: There's no reward for love. You've given him everything he's capable of receiving . . . He's had his thrill.

BET: His thrill?

DORA: You.

BET: You're twisting a knife in my heart.

DORA: Not I, Dewi. Every woman's love is a knife in the heart.

BET: He gave me his word, his word and his hands.

DORA: He'll never forgive you.

BET: Because I phoned? . . . As we arranged?

DORA: It's a pity he has to wake up.
(John enters in his minister's clothing)

JOHN: Bet! As early as this! Bad news?

DORA: John, the police are on their way here from town.

JOHN: Oh no!

DORA: They're coming to fetch him.

JOHN: Does he know?

DORA: He's sleeping heavily.

JOHN: Good heavens! . . . *(He looks through the window)* They'll take ten minutes from town in that big car . . . I wonder if it isn't best to tell him?

DORA: That would drive him out of his mind — there's nothing to be gained by that. The shorter the goodbyes the better.

JOHN: Why did you decide so suddenly to call the police? . . . You changed your mind?

BET: I'm the one phoned the inspector, Mr Rhys.

JOHN: *(in surprise and fear)* I didn't dare. I didn't dare although I knew it would save him.

BET: That's what you begged me to do last night.

JOHN: I didn't love him enough . . . You do.

DORA: At least now there are things to be done and plans to be made for him.

JOHN: We need to get a lawyer to go to the station and be with him while they're questioning him.

DORA: The same one as before?

JOHN: Who better? They'll take him to England afterwards. That's where he struck the traveller.

DORA: Is there a chance you can be free to go there, Bet?

BET: For the trial?

DORA: Instead of his father and me. It's important that one of us is there to support him.

BET: I'm afraid to look one day ahead. I'm afraid of every promise now.
(Each in turn throughout this conversation goes to the window to look out - no one is able to be calm.)

167

JOHN: Bet is right. There's no need to rush.

DORA: If the police are on their way here, there'll be quite a rush when they arrive.

JOHN: There's the worry of arranging to get help for him —

BET: It's better than screaming.

JOHN: It helps one not to scream.

DORA: We're all on edge, everyone but Dewi, keeping our ears open for the sound of the car.

BET: Like people waiting for someone to die, and chattering.

JOHN: Lord, have mercy on him.

DORA: I'd like to take him breakfast before they arrive. Is that a risk?

JOHN: They'll give him a proper breakfast in town. The question is who is to wake him up, us or them?

DORA: Us, of course . . . Bet.

JOHN: Once the police are in the house, they'll be the ones in charge here.

DORA: They won't go upstairs without permission?

JOHN: They're not coming here to sympathize.

DORA: But this is our house.

JOHN: Until they arrive.

DORA: If that's the case Bet can wake him up and take him a cup of tea. It would be dreadfully cruel to let a policeman wake him here in his own home.

JOHN: Dora dear, don't lose your head.

DORA: A cup of tea?

JOHN: It's wrong for us to wake him now.

DORA: You're the one who first talked of waking him.

JOHN: Yes, before I'd considered it.

BET: *(at the window)* I can't bear this.

JOHN: *(to Dora)* We must not kill him.

DORA: I want to spare him any more fright than is necessary.

JOHN: Then let him sleep.

DORA: But the police?

JOHN: The police can wake him.

DORA: By putting the cuffs on his hands!

JOHN: That's what will save his life.

BET: *(turning agitatedly from the window)* Save his life? No one here is a threat to his life. He's my love. I've just come from his arms.

DORA: To call the Philistines to take him.

JOHN: He threatened his own life.

BET: He did?

JOHN: Last night, here.

BET: That's over now. We've made our vows to each other. A second start in life. A new life and a new Wales in faith and love.

JOHN: Last night though?

BET: Yes, last night.

JOHN: Last night is last night to Dewi. Yesterday is yesterday. They won't exist for him today. To him Welsh has no word that connects yesterday to today.

DORA: We're like a band of murderers plotting to betray him.

BET: You're putting the blame on me. Because I phoned. I had to. That was the agreement, that was the condition. Oh, what will I do?

DORA: I was going to phone myself, this morning.

JOHN: We're all to blame, all of us. Even Dewi.

BET: Last night we planned the future. Planned to marry.

JOHN: There's no knowing what we'll plan today.

BET: He's your son.

JOHN: I can't die in his place.

DORA: Be quiet, John. You're saying dangerous things.

BET: You're spitting on my love. You're killing Dewi in my heart.

JOHN: That's what I would do if I could. That's my duty. Before he wakes up.

BET: I'll go wake him now.

JOHN: Why now?

BET: To prove my faith in him.

JOHN: The time to wake him was before you called the police.

BET: I know that. I didn't dare. I dare now.
(She starts to go)

DORA: *(at the window)* Here they are— The car is here.

BET: Dewi! . . . Oh, Dewi!

DORA: Four of them. The Inspector with the driver, and two in the back. They're here.

BET: At least he had last night.

JOHN: There's room for three in the back.

DORA: And his hands bound between them. Oh if I could just see him go.

(A heavy knocking on the house door. John goes through the centre door and leaves it wide open. The two women stand on the right.)

DORA: Bet.

BET: Yes?

DORA: Whatever happens now, keep your self-respect. Without that love is in vain.

(Evans comes to the door and calls back)

EVANS: Paul, the back . . . Hughes, stay there, the front door . . . *(Evans comes in and Jones after him; then John)* . . . Good morning, Ma'am. Well, Mr Rhys, the message arrived. We were expecting it. Thank you for not wasting much time . . . Where is he?

JOHN: In his bed, sleeping.

EVANS: We'll have to wake him up.

DORA: Not you, Mr Evans, me.

EVANS: He's not at home, Ma'am, but on the run from his proper place. It's our duty to get him back there without delay.

JOHN: Inspector, he asked us to call you here himself. He explained to us the attack of nerves that made him escape. He's putting himself back in your hands voluntarily, quite soon after he reached his home. I think that remembering and considering all this is a sufficient reason for listening to his mother's request.

EVANS: Mr Rhys, the lad is not just a runaway prisoner. He's a runaway prisoner who has also stolen a car and money, and attacked an innocent man and half-killed him.

DORA: How is the traveller, Mr Evans?

EVANS: The news last night was that he's getting over it.

DORA: Then he wasn't half-killed?

EVANS: A quite serious injury.

JOHN: That is a terrible concern and sadness to us.

DORA: Before I go to call him, may I ask one thing of you, Mr Evans?

EVANS: Anything possible, Ma'am, anything possible.

DORA: Since he's the one putting himself in your hands, can you take him without my having to see his hands in cuffs?

EVANS: Everything's fine, Mrs Rhys, if he'll come quietly. He isn't likely to knock four of us down. He can sit between the two constables in the back of the car as if he were going to his wedding. Anything else?

DORA: Nothing else. I'll go up to him now.
(But the middle door opens and Dewi, in a dressing gown over his pyjamas, stands there, looking at the company and laughing pleasantly)

DEWI: Well! Well! Who would have thought it! in the minister's house! . . .
(singing, with a gesture of leading the singing) . . . "Here's a very joyous gathering . . ." Come on, Jones, join in the hymn.
(Jones pulls the cuffs from his pocket but Evans raises a hand to stop him)

EVANS: Are you coming with us quietly, Dewi Rhys?

DEWI: I came down for the sole purpose of giving you a welcome, Inspector. I heard the loud knocking on the door of the house. No one but policemen and gypsy women knock like that. So I knew that my old friends had arrived. One must be hospitable, I said, preserve the good name of the manse, and down I came to greet you . . . Welcome, coppers!

EVANS: If you'll come at once without any tricks, I've promised your mother that you may walk to the car with your hands free.

DEWI: At once?

EVANS: Yes, at once.

DEWI: Without a bath, without shaving, without dressing, without breakfast? My dear Inspector, you can't do things that way in a minister's house.

EVANS; We'll give you breakfast at the station. Where are your prison clothes?

DEWI: In the best wardrobe with my father's preaching suit. Birds of a feather, you know.

EVANS: We have a new charge against you. You know that?

DEWI: Serious?

EVANS: You can judge that at the station.

DEWI: You know, Dad, the odd thing with these policemen is that they never grow up. They go on with their children's games to the last minute.

171

EVANS: I'll give you four minutes to dress. If you're not here by then Constable Jones will come to fetch you.

DEWI: Thank you, friend. But before I go may I ask a question or two of my family here and Miss Edward who's with them?

EVANS: Be quick.

DEWI: I'll come straight to the point . . . Who's the serpent who betrayed me?

DORA: You're the one doing the betraying, Dewi. I called the Inspector.

DEWI: My darling mother! To prove your love, I suppose.

DORA: To save you.

DEWI: Well, it's a bit of comfort that *she* didn't do it.

BET: Dewi!

DEWI: A voice! A voice from the past!

BET: That is how you keep a vow?

DEWI: A vow?

BET: Last night.

DEWI: Last night? . . . When was last night? . . . Ah! I see! *You* called the police?

BET: Yes. Me.

DEWI: And Mam as usual not knowing the difference between true and false, telling a lie to spare pain.

BET: I could kill you for saying that.

DEWI: You've killed me already . . . *(A gesture towards the police)* Here's the funeral. Your final favour.

BET: Is nothing sacred with you?

DEWI: Sacred? What does that mean?

BET: *(slowly)* Something that's lost now forever.

DEWI: *(quietly, scornfully)* Pretty good, my girl. You've hit the bottom at last. Father, mother, country, language, love, those are your shibboleths, aren't they? It's all babble. And you and your sneaky little betrayal, and your slipping out of bed to call the police before I woke up and prevented you, so that you could have the thrill of saving me and have the romance of marriage at the prison door, — you saw yourself as a guardian angel, didn't you? You know, there's not a shred of meaning to your existence. Nothing but self-deceit and the lust of the flesh pretending to make a sacrifice. You're an accident, an accident leading to an accident.

172

There's only one thing left that's not accidental. So go hang yourself, you nightmare!

(Dewi exits and goes upstairs)

EVANS: Keep this door open, Jones, and keep your eye on the stairs. We'll give him exactly four minutes. Which is his room, Mrs Rhys?

DORA: The second on the left.

EVANS: Are you prepared to answer a question or two, Mr Rhys?

JOHN: Now?

EVANS: This minute.

JOHN: If I can.

EVANS: When did he arrive here?

JOHN: Last night.

EVANS: And the hour?

JOHN: About half-past seven.

EVANS: Who let him in?

JOHN: No one. That window was open. We only lock it before we go for our holidays. And he knows that. So he came in.

EVANS: He was here in the house when the constable called at about eight o'clock?

JOHN: Yes.

EVANS: And you knew that?

JOHN: No, I didn't. But if I had known, I wouldn't have answered any differently at the time.

EVANS: What might have been doesn't matter. The Constable came here again at about eleven?

JOHN: Yes.

EVANS: And you knew by then that he was in the house?

JOHN: We had talked at length about the situation, he and I.

EVANS: Although you'd promised to call the police on the telephone the minute you saw him?

JOHN: Just so. In spite of the promise.

EVANS: The Constable explained to you the danger from the standpoint of the law?

JOHN: Mr Jones did his duty.

EVANS: You didn't say a word to him about the lad being in the house?

JOHN: Not a word.

EVANS: Why not?

JOHN: Because I had promised Dewi that he would get a night's sleep here in his home before giving himself up to the police in the morning.

EVANS: A night's sleep?

JOHN: After a rather troubled day.

EVANS: Did he get a night's sleep, Miss Edward?

BET: You are asking me?

EVANS: Yes.

BET: My father knows the Chief Constable well, and he will hear about your question and the slander that's in it.

EVANS: I'm suggesting that you came to him here last night at about ten o'clock and kept him on his feet until very late.

BET: The Chief Constable and my father's lawyer can judge the meaning of your question.

EVANS: *(angry)* You were with him here when the Constable called last night. Isn't that true?

BET: Put on another cap, have you Inspector?

JONES: Four minutes are up, sir.

EVANS: *(furiously)* Go up to him. The second door on the left. And bring the vicious little cub with you just as he is, in cuffs if you must.
           (Jones runs up the stairs and Evans stands in the door to watch him. We hear knocking and kicking the door and the voice of Jones.)

JONES: The door is locked.

EVANS: Locked?
           (Evans runs up. We hear the door broken in, then Evans runs down to the parlour door.)

EVANS: The room is empty. Where can he be?

JOHN: The attic. There's a window there that opens onto the roof. Come on!
           (John and Evans run up, John shouting "Dewi! Dewi!" Two constables appear outside through the window, shouting and looking up. Dora opens the window to lean out. Bet is on the right side of the window. John runs out and shouts through the window)

JOHN: He's on the roof! On the edge of the roof! Not dressed!
           (Dora runs outside. Everyone is outside except Bet, and shouting)

ALL: Dewi, don't! . . . Don't do it boy! . . . Go back!
(There is a general outcry, and the shadow of the young man's body falls across the window. Silence for a moment, then busy movement. The Inspector enters and telephones. Dora enters and after her two constables carrying Dewi's body.)

DORA: He's had his final thrill.

CURTAIN

ON THE TRAIN

(Yn y Trên, 1965)

Yn y Trên was first performed on radio for the Welsh Home Service on 8 May, 1965. In a chronological ordering of the plays it should therefore precede *Cymru Fydd, Tomorrow's Wales*, which it may be said to anticipate. I have thought it better, however, to present Saunders Lewis' "triad" as an uninterrupted sequence, with *On the Train* serving as a *coda*, a dramatized metaphor — which the playwright has said was suggested by a passage in Jean-Paul Startre's autobiography *Les Mots* — that conveys the quintessence of the triad.

The script that follows is my adaptation of the play for staging. It was performed by theatre students at Marymount Manhattan College under my direction in December 1975 in a programme of three short contemporary plays expressive of three different cultures. (The other two were N. F. Simpson's *A Resounding Tinkle* and Derek Walcott's *Malcochon*.) The dialogue of the original radio play has been translated unaltered; the stage directions are mine.

There have been enough terminations of rail service in the United States for the central situation to be immediately accessible. But I thought it essential to prepare an American audience for the Welsh setting unfamiliar to most of them, including the very existence of the Welsh language, and for particular references in the script. I therefore devised a "prologue" using slides, voice-overs, and recorded songs. This seemed to be effective in providing both information and an initial mood and tone, and I have included it, as well as noted specific recordings used at key moments in the play itself, as of possible value for any future stage productions. Statements by the "Saunders Lewis Voice" are taken from his article on "Welsh Writers and Nationalism" and his speech on "The Fate of

178

the Language"; the "radio announcements", based on newspaper reports, are my own invention, and do not quote actual radio broadcasts.

When the play was printed in *Barn* (August 1965), Saunders Lewis added this postscript: "I ask the reader not to accept the Guard's judgment as a final verdict on the Traveller. The Traveller is probably as sane and sensible as you or I — or the Guard."

CHARACTERS

A Traveller
A British Railways Guard

The set requires a large screen which can be lowered and raised downstage centre on which slides can be projected (preferably from behind), and a suitably modified version of an old-fashioned first-class British train compartment, with the exterior door containing a window that pulls up to shut on the upstage side and a short segment of the corridor running past the interior doorway on the downstage side, designed and positioned to allow the Guard to enter and exit stage right.

       *   *   *   *

On a screen downstage centre a series of slides of Welsh places and faces, with recurrent slides of empty railway stations and unused track, accompanied by the following music and statements. The music begins each segment, is held long enough to establish itself, then fades behind the voice, and is brought up again after the statement before being faded out as the music for the following segment rises.

1. Music: "Cymru" ("Wales"), a celebratory poem by Gwenallt sung by Meinir Lloyd to counterpointed harp accompaniment by Morfudd Maesaleg, an example of the traditional Welsh art of *penillion* singing. (From *Meinir Lloyd yn canu penillion*.)
    Statement ("Saunders Lewis voice"): "Civilization must be more than an abstraction. It must have a local habitation and a name. Here, its name is Wales."

179

2. Music: "The Trumpet Shall Sound (And the Dead Shall Be Raised)", an excerpt from Handel's *Messiah*, long a favourite oratorio for Welsh choral groups, sung by Geraint Evans accompanied by the BBC Welsh Orchestra. (From *The Artistry of Geraint Evans.*)

   Statement ("Radio announcer voice"): "Her Highness the Duchess of Kent officiated yesterday at the opening of the new Mental Hospital in Carmarthen. Princess Alexandra noted that with this modern facility Britain was assured of the finest health care in the world."

3. Music: "Dw' isio bod yn Sais" ("I want to be an Englishman"), a satiric Welsh "pop" song composed and performed by Huw Jones.

   Statement ("Saunders Lewis voice"): "The Welsh nation may be dying of indifference and sloth."

4. Music: "Hen Wlad Fy Nhadau" ("Land of My Fathers"), the Welsh national anthem, sung by the Rhos Male Voice Choir. (From *Music from the Welsh Mines.*)

   Statement ("Radio announcer voice"): "Parliament has approved the plan submitted by Dr Richard Beeching, Chairman of the British Rail Board, for rationalising the present system of rail service. The Beeching Plan calls for the gradual termination of more than 2,000 passenger stations. It is anticipated that within five years there will be no passenger service in most of Wales. The South Wales line between Carmarthen and Aberystwyth will be closed next year."

5. Music: "Ar Hyd y Nos" ("All Through the Night"), sung by Thomas L. Thomas. (From *Welsh Traditional Song.*)

   Statement ("Saunders Lewis voice"): "Welsh will end as a living language, should the present trend continue, about the beginning of the twenty-first century, assuming that there will be people left in the island of Britain at that time."

Lights fade to black on the last slide, and in the darkness the screen is raised and the compartment wheeled into position downstage centre. As the last harp notes fade on the final song of the Prologue, from the darkness we hear the sound of a train arriving at a station, doors opening and closing, people moving hurriedly, and a porter shouting "Carmarthen, Carmarthen".

Then we hear a young woman's voice announcing: "The train now standing at platform one is the six-ten train for Aberystwyth, stopping at all stations between Carmarthen and Aberystwyth."

The sound of train doors and people moving. A porter calls, "Aberystwyth train".

The young woman's voice again, but this time uncertainly: "The train now standing . . . now standing at . . . at platform one . . . is the ten minutes past six . . ."

We hear the guard's whistle, doors closing . . . the young woman's voice as if from far away uncertain and fading . . . in the distance like an echo: "The six-ten for Aberystwyth . . . stopping . . . stopping . . ."

GUARD: *(offstage, in darkness)* Aberystwyth train!
(A long whistle. We hear a door open and close with a bang. We hear the train start, and the guard's door close with a bang. We hear the train noise as it departs, then lowered to remain in the background throughout the play. Light comes up on the first-class compartment as the Traveller, who has entered it from upstage in darkness, is closing the outer door and raising the window. The light should suggest the end of day, and should be very gradually faded as the play progresses, in keeping with the references to this in the dialogue.)

181

TRAVELLER: *(sitting, looking around the compartment, then out the window)*
Well! Well! . . . Nothing to spare! . . . Touch and go!
. . . . A compartment all to myself . . . First class . . .
No newspaper . . . Nothing to read . . . Not to worry
. . . The countryside is pleasant . . . Half an hour till
nightfall . . . There's the river . . . Strange too . . . very
strange . . . Travelling in a train . . . in Wales . . . and
night ahead of me . . . Travelling towards night . . .
The night of Wales . . .

GUARD: *(offstage right)* Tickets please — *Tocynnau.*
(The Guard enters right and walks along the corridor to the compartment door.)

GUARD: Good evening, sir.

TRAVELLER: The same to you, and many of them. Is it going to rain?

GUARD: I think so. Those clouds are threatening. Showers, you know. March is about gone.

TRAVELLER: That clump of primroses there, close to the rail, proves that you're right.

GUARD: Yes, there they are every spring, in the nook near the rail.

TRAVELLER: Please, sit down, I'll be glad of your company.

GUARD: *(sitting opposite the Traveller)* Well, for a minute, sir. Then to work. I'm collecting tickets.

TRAVELLER: Really. Interesting. Like collecting stamps, eh? Have you a good collection, a valuable collection?

GUARD: *(with a soft laugh, politely)* It's the Government gets the value, not me.

TAVELLER: You know, this collecting craze is a strange thing. There are all kinds of us. I too am a collector.

GUARD: What do you collect, sir?

TRAVELLER: Not train tickets.

GUARD: That isn't hard to believe.

TRAVELLER: Try to guess.

GUARD: Do you drive a car, a motor car?

TRAVELLER: No indeed. Do you think I collect cars?

GUARD: No, not exactly. I was thinking you might be collecting summonses.

TRAVELLER: Did you ever sit or lie in the grass? In those fields? See them?

GUARD: It's quite a spell since I went courting, sir.

TRAVELLER: If you lay down in the grass and examined it, what would you see?

GUARD: What would I see? Grass, I suppose.

TRAVELLER: But what kind of grass?

GUARD: Are there kinds of grass?

TRAVELLER: My dear fellow, where did you go to school?

GUARD: Carmarthenshire, of course.

TRAVELLER: When I was a lad of ten I sat in a field near my house. I had a dog and the dog was sick: he had the look of death on him. Close to the spot where I sat down to cry I saw a rather large cluster of clover. I said to myself, if I find a four-leaf clover, Carlo will get better. I started to search. In a second I found a four-leaf clover. They're a sure sign of good luck, that everything's all right. Ever since that time I collect them.

GUARD: Do you have many?

TRAVELLER: Just that one. I've never found another.

GUARD: *(laughing a bit)* But you collect them?

TRAVELLER: I was a child. I hadn't come to the train.

GUARD: It's not very often you find clover in a train. You have a better chance collecting tickets for the Government.

TRAVELLER: That's your luck. You are the Government's deputy on the train.

GUARD: I hadn't thought of it like that.

TRAVELLER: A responsible position.

GUARD: A tidy little job. Not much pay. And there's no knowing how long the position will last these days.

TRAVELLER: But *you* are the Government on the train. That must be a comfort?

GUARD: A bit of a servant to everyone, that's how I see myself.

TRAVELLER: Tut, tut. Don't talk like the Pope. After all, you're only a guard.

GUARD: *(rising)* And I must get to work. May I see your ticket, sir?

TRAVELLER: Ticket? *You* collect tickets That's what you said, isn't it?

183

GUARD: That's my job.

TRAVELLER: A train ticket, yes?

GUARD: A train ticket, sir.

TRAVELLER: But I can't help you at all. I've never collected them.

GUARD: A ticket for this trip, sir, on this train.

TRAVELLER: Is a ticket needed for this train?

GUARD: One must have a ticket to travel.

TRAVELLER: *I* am travelling.

GUARD: There's no doubt about it.

TRAVELLER: But I have no ticket.

GUARD: That's all right, sir. You reached the station in a hurry, of course, with no time to purchase a ticket.

TRAVELLER: Why need one purchase a ticket?

GUARD: Quite right, when you can pay on the train. My notion is that if everyone paid the guard it would save a lot of expense. The way the buses do.

TRAVELLER: Have you told that to Doctor Beeching?

GUARD: Who is Doctor Beeching?

TRAVELLER: Isn't he the minister in charge of Welsh affairs?

GUARD: *(sitting again and taking out his book)* Where are you going, sir?

TRAVELLER: I'm not going anywhere.

GUARD: *(with a friendly little laugh)* Just so. It's the train that's going. Rather good, sir. Here's my book. A one-way ticket from Carmarthen to Aberystywth, is it? First-class, one way.

TRAVELLER: Is this train going to Aberystwyth?

GUARD: This is the Aberystwyth train. You came on in Carmarthen.

TRAVELLER: Everyone must start somewhere, I suppose.

GUARD: How long were you in Carmarthen, sir? . . . . They're performing miracles there, I've heard. Very respectable people go there of their own free will. Returning to Aberystwyth, are you? A college professor, is it? The strain was too great.

TRAVELLER: I am going on the train, going along with the train. There's no choice once you're on the train, is there?

GUARD: When on the train, one must go with the train.

TRAVELLER: But the train can stop.

184

GUARD: Oh yes, yes, the train can stop.

TRAVELLER: Then one can get off.

GUARD: Sure enough. After paying for a ticket. A ticket to where, sir? I must move on.

TRAVELLER: Move on? You can't move ahead of the train.

GUARD: I go along the train to collect tickets. That's my job.

TRAVELLER: Why? Are there other people on the train?

GUARD: I hope so.

TRAVELLER: You hope so? Don't you know? Have you seen any?

GUARD: *(laughing)* To tell the truth, no. I leapt on at the last minute. The doors had closed and the train had started. It's enjoyable.

TRAVELLER: What's enjoyable?

GUARD: Finding the passengers, asking for tickets, catching an occasional sly dog . . . First class, Carmarthen to Aberystwyth, eh sir?

TRAVELLER: *You* know best. If that's the system, everything's fine.

GUARD: *You* know where you're going, sir.

TRAVELLER: Me? How could I know? I'm not the one driving the train.

GUARD: No, that's true.

TRAVELLER: Where are the other passengers going? If there are other passengers. Don't you know?

GUARD: I haven't seen their tickets.

TRAVELLER: There's no knowing.

GUARD: No, there's no knowing.

TRAVELLER: And so there's no way to purchase a ticket.

GUARD: Not without knowing.

TRAVELLER: And yet here they all are on the train, going without knowing where.

GUARD: But they have tickets.

TRAVELLER: How do you know? Have you seen them?

GUARD: I haven't seen them. I'm presuming. Believing. That's the usual thing.
            (The train sound comes slowly up through the next speeches, accompanied by the Welsh "pop" song "Dwyn y lein" ["Taking the line"], composed and sung by Meic Stevens.)

185

TRAVELLER: A station! Here's a station!

GUARD: Bronwydd Arms.

TRAVELLER: Bronwydd Arms? The train stops at Bronwydd Arms. The train stops at all stations . . . *(Shouting)* It's not stopping . . . Why doesn't it stop? Stop it! *You're* the guard!

GUARD: There's no station at Bronwydd Arms any more. *(Train sound down. Song faded and out.)*

TRAVELLER: There's no station. Why?

GUARD: For the same reason you were in Carmarthen.

TRAVELLER: To get the old country back on its feet?

GUARD: Now, sir, I must fill out this ticket. Carmarthen to Aberystwyth, is that right?

TRAVELLER: *(warily)* Is there a station at Aberystwyth?

GUARD: Yes, yes. There's a station there.

TRAVELLER: Does the train stop at the station there?

GUARD: Oh, no.

TRAVELLER: And you said that this is the Aberystwyth line!

GUARD: That's right.

TRAVELLER: So the train *must* stop there?

GUARD: It can't.

TRAVELLER: It can't?

GUARD: Floods. A fortnight back. Part of the track was swept away by the current . . . Between Ystrad Fflur and Trawsgoed.

TRAVELLER: *(quietly threatening)* Look, Mr Guard, did you come here intending to trick me?

GUARD: I came here to collect tickets. You do not have a ticket. I am prepared to sell you a ticket. That's all. That's the law. Travelling on the train without a ticket is breaking the law. You rich people think, you in first class, that you can spit on the rules of the railroad. You can't . . . A ticket to where, sir, — Aberystwyth?

TRAVELLER: Are you prepared to give me a train ticket to Aberystwyth?

GUARD: This minute.

TRAVELLER: And you know that the train can never reach Aberystwyth? Does it go over the cliff at Caradog

	Falls? Are you offering me a ticket to death and damnation . . . because I'm travelling first class?
GUARD:	Now, sir, take it easy. The train will stop at Tregaron. There will be a bus there at the station to take you safely the rest of the way to Aberystwyth.
TRAVELLER:	Like that, is it?
GUARD:	The railway takes care of you nicely to the end of the journey.
TRAVELLER:	Is there first class on the bus?
GUARD:	Hardly.
TRAVELLER:	And you want me to pay for first class to Aberystwyth. Ha! Ha!
GUARD:	Right-oh then. I'll give you a ticket to Tregaron. You can pay on the bus for the rest of the trip.
TRAVELLER:	I don't want a ticket to Tregaron. Do I look like a poacher?
GUARD:	I've told you: the train can't go any farther.
TRAVELLER:	Why hasn't the track been repaired?
GUARD:	Ask heaven!
TRAVELLER:	No, I must have an answer. Who is responsible?
GUARD:	Not me.
TRAVELLER:	That's what everyone says: "Who's responsible? Not me." Ask the people who are on this train — if there are people on this train — and that's what each one will say: Not me.
GUARD:	That's probably the truth.
TRAVELLER:	The truth? My dear man, if that's the truth and everyone says it, then everyone's mad.
GUARD:	How long were you in hospital, sir?
	(The train sound comes slowly up through the next speeches, accompanied by "Can y Milgi" ["Song of the Greyhound"], a popular children's song recorded by members of The Welsh League of Youth on Urdd Camping Songs.*)*
TRAVELLER:	*(shouting)* A station! Here's a station!
GUARD:	Cynwyl Elfed.
TRAVELLER	*(Rising and continuing to shout excitedly)* The train isn't stopping! It's supposed to stop! It must stop!

GUARD: There's no station at Cynwyl any more.

TRAVELLER: *(still shouting)* The train is going through. Look . . . There's the platform, there's the name, Cynwyl, there's the office, there's the "gents". There *is* a station! Stop the train! Stop it!

GUARD: I can't stop the train.

(Train sound down. Song faded and out.)

TRAVELLER: *(falling back into his seat)* What did you say?

GUARD: I can't stop the train.

TRAVELLER: *(solemnly)* On your oath — you can't?

GUARD: That isn't my job.

TRAVELLER: If that's the case, how can you sell me a ticket to Tregaron?

GUARD: That *is* my job.

TRAVELLER: Is there any connection between your job and the train?

GUARD: There you are, sir. *(As he finishes writing the ticket)* Carmarthen to Tregaron, first class one way. Fifteen shillings, please.

TRAVELLER: Slowly, friend. Is there a station at Tregaron?

GUARD: Yes, yes. A model station.

TRAVELLER: The same kind as at Cynwyl Elfed?

GUARD: A larger station. Tregaron is a market town.

TRAVELLER: And since there's a station at Tregaron, this train stops there?

GUARD: Yes, yes, sure to.

TRAVELLER: Do you *know* that the train stops there?

GUARD: Know? Well now, it's not possible to know for sure before it happens.

TRAVELLER: So you don't know?

GUARD: I'm fairly certain.

TRAVELLER: But you don't *know*?

GUARD: How can I?

TRAVELLER: And nevertheless you're trying to sell me a fifteen-shilling ticket to go to a market town where you don't know that the train stops?

GUARD: Nonsense! I have every reason to believe that this train stops at Tregaron.

TRAVELLER: I had every reason to believe that it was stopping at

188

Bronwydd Arms. It didn't stop. And since it didn't stop, there wasn't a station there, you said. Then I had every reason to believe for sure that it would stop at Cynwyl Elfed. On went the train. There wasn't a station there either you said . . . and I planned to get off at Cynwyl Elfed.

GUARD: Get off at Cynwyl! You didn't say one word about getting off at Cynwyl. You asked for a ticket to Aberystwyth.

TRAVELLER: Me? I have never in my life dreamed of buying a ticket to Aberystwyth. No one ever went to Aberystwyth unless they had to.

GUARD: Good heavens! And what was your business at Cynwyl Elfed if I may be so bold?

TRAVELLER: My business at Cynwyl? To get off the train. It looked like a pleasant little place to get off the train.

GUARD: Did you have other business there?

TRAVELLER: What other business is possible for a person on a train?

GUARD: But after arriving?

TRAVELLER: Yes, what then? After arriving, as we've seen, the great achievement is to stay. There's no way. We've kept going on. One must go along with the train on the train. The train's destiny is our destiny. There's no stopping. It's a trip with no purpose but the train's purpose. There's no escape. We see an attractive little station, a place of quiet, a small empty heaven, and decide to raise a tent there, where neither poisonous spider nor member of parliament ever comes. But on goes the train, on to Caradog Falls and the dreadful cliff and the meaningless end.

GUARD: If you had said that you wanted to get off at Cynwyl, there would have been a way of arranging it.

TRAVELLER: Said? Said to whom? When?

GUARD: Before starting. To the station master at Carmarthen or the superintendent.

TRAVELLER: Please, Mr Guard, don't talk so stupidly. I hadn't seen Cynwyl Elfed then. Upon seeing that enchanting haven, upon going past, upon missing it, I decided to

	stay there. You must try to understand: I'm a person, a person. Not a computer.
GUARD:	If that's the case, you have no excuse. You must pay for the trip to Tregaron. Fifteen shillings, sir.
TRAVELLER:	It isn't the price that's important. The price is neither here nor there.
GUARD:	*(laughing)* It's a fortunate thing to be able to say that. Most people grumble about the high prices.
TRAVELLER:	But they pay?
GUARD:	To the last farthing. We make sure that there's a policeman around the terminus as a precaution.
TRAVELLER:	Proper enough. Is Tregaron a terminus?
GUARD:	Yes, for the time being, for now.
TRAVELER:	Is there a policeman there?
GUARD:	A giant of a man, from Cardiganshire.
TRAVELLER:	One of Tregaron's boyos?
GUARD:	He has a grip like steel.
TRAVELLER:	How many stations are there before reaching Tregaron?
GUARD:	There are no stations before reaching it. Every one of the other stations has been closed.
TRAVELLER:	Look here, Mr Guard, I'm not joking. I must get off before reaching Tregaron.
GUARD:	I'm sorry, sir, but you can't. There's no help for it.
TRAVELLER:	I must be able to, I must.
GUARD:	Why must you?
TRAVELLER:	Because there are only two choices ahead of me: a court of law and prison at Tregaron or a fall and annihilation over the cliff at Caradog Falls.
GUARD:	*(on his feet)* So you're a criminal, are you?
TRAVELLER:	I haven't a brass farthing to my name.
GUARD:	You're one of those, are you?
TRAVELLER:	A person, not a computer
GUARD:	And you chose first class as well.
TRAVELLER:	Chose? Don't blaspheme. Even though you are the deputy for the Government. I never had a choice. I was put on the train.
GUARD:	Put on by whom, you trash?
TRAVELLER:	How do I know by whom or why? Perhaps it was a

joke, or an accident, I don't know. The Aberystwyth line too, to the moon and beyond. A railway decaying, a country wasting away, every station dead, and night closing in on us . . . Please, light the compartment so I can see where I am.

GUARD: You haven't any right to a light. You can't pay for where you are. You'd better get used to darkness. Your prison will be dark.

(The train sound comes slowly up during the following speeches, accompanied by the lullaby "Si Hei Lwli", sung by Meredydd Evans on Welsh Traditional Songs.*)*

TRAVELLER: *(rising)* A station! . . . Another station, by heaven!

GUARD: Llanpumsaint.

TRAVELLER: Right-oh then, stop it! I'll get off here . . . Stop it.

GUARD: I can't stop it.

TRAVELLER: Damn you, I can. There's a signal cord above your head. Pull it.

GUARD: There's a five-pound fine for pulling it.

TRAVELLER: What's the difference! I'm already a bankrupt!
(He pulls the cord.)

GUARD: You're making your punishment worse.

TRAVELLER: There now! I've pulled it . . . Now! . . . Now for it!

GUARD: You see? We're passing the station. There's no light in the office. The train is picking up speed. On we go, on, on.

(Train sound down. Song faded and out.)

TRAVELLER: *(sinking back into his seat)* But I pulled the cord.

GUARD: That cord is out of order. It doesn't reach the engine. Pull as often as you like, the train goes on to Tregaron. You've been caught, my lad.

TRAVELLER: We're going like fury.

GUARD: A diesel engine.

TRAVELLER: You can't see the hedges any more. It's night. I can scarcely see you.

GUARD: I'm between you and the door. You can't escape to the corridor.

TRAVELLER: I'm glad of your company since all of us are lost . . . It would be a dreadful thing to be all by yourself on the train, guilty, without a penny in your pocket to pay,

191

and the train rushing towards night, towards Caradog
Falls and the cliff.

GUARD: This train is going no farther than Tregaron. You'll
have to explain to the magistrate there how you came
on the train without a ticket.

TRAVELLER: I'm not the first.

GUARD: That's no excuse.

TRAVELLER: Yes, it is. It's something inherited.

GUARD: Being without a ticket?

TRAVELLER: Of course. Two hundred and fifty million years ago my
family was sleeping nicely on top of the ocean, and
suddenly, you see, the tide had turned and the ebb had
left them on a patch of seaweed and mud, on dry land,
or half dry. And that's where they were, caught . . .
without a ticket . . . We're ticketless to this day. . .
*(A long whistle from the train engine . . . A moment of
silence . . . then long and loud, almost mad laughter
from Traveller.)*

GUARD: What's wrong with you, man? Are you out of your
mind? Why that crazy laughter? Shut up!

TRAVELLER: Don't worry, dear brother . . . Ha-ha-ha-ha-ha! . . . .
Don't be afraid. It's as clear as daylight even though
night's upon us here. Ha-ha-ha!

GUARD: What is it you see so clearly?

TRAVELLER: Just that all this anxiety . . . this failure to pay . . . and
that giant of a Cardi at Tregaron station . . . the guilty
fear . . .

GUARD: What about them?

TRAVELLER: My dear fellow, they're nothing but the bogies of
night. They don't exist. There's no meaning to a train
ticket. It would be much better for you to collect four-
leaf clovers.

GUARD: You'll see when we come to Tregaron.

TRAVELLER: Look here. Can you see me?

GUARD: I can see your shape.

TRAVELLER: Right-oh then. Now. Do you believe that this train
will stop at Tregaron station?

GUARD: I do.

TRAVELLER: Why?

GUARD:	That's how it's been arranged.
TRAVELLER:	Can the train stop there?
GUARD:	The driver can stop it.
TRAVELLER:	Have you seen the driver?
GUARD:	I came on the train late.
TRAVELLER:	The signal cord doesn't reach the driver?
GUARD:	No.
TRAVELLER:	Have you seen one sign that there is a driver on the train?
GUARD:	Isn't the train moving? That's the proof.
TRAVELLER:	My boy, my boy, you *are* an innocent.
GUARD:	A train cannot go without a driver.
TRAVELLER:	You know nothing at all about this electronic world. The train is most safe, most secure, *without* a driver. In the pure engine there's no room for failure or misjudgment. That's the secret of the train. It cannot miss or change its course, it just stays on the track. Everything will be fine until Caradog Falls ... Because there's no driver. That's why there's no connecting cord. There's no one for it to be connected with. There's no brake. And so, dear brother, there's no need of a ticket. You see, the train isn't going anywhere. Just going, going, going, through the endless night and the dark and dead stations.
GUARD:	You're deranged, man, you're mad!
TRAVELLER:	Of course I'm mad. That is why I'm on the train. That's the kind of train it is. But I'm not mad enough to collect tickets.
GUARD:	When we reach Tregaron, we shall see who's mad.
TRAVELLER:	You Nazi devil! Do you think that the end of the line is Belsen or Dachau?
GUARD:	*(shouting suddenly)* The end of the journey is not Caradog Falls!
TRAVELLER:	*(laughing triumphantly)* You're afraid! Afraid that the train doesn't stop.
GUARD:	I want to go home at the end of the trip.
TRAVELLER:	You want to return to the womb: Tell that to the driver! Ha, ha, ha!
	(The Traveller lowers the compartment window. The

193

light fades to black during the following dialogue. The train sound comes up immediately on the lowering of the window, accompanied more slowly by the rising sound of "Diadem", the traditional Welsh hymn familiar in English as "All hail the power of Jesus' name" – the refrain in Welsh means "God is love" –, recorded in A Nation Sings, *a gymanfa ganu held at the Royal Albert Hall.)*

GUARD: Why are you opening the window? The night wind is cold.

TRAVELLER: It's impossible to go home, brother. But a person can choose the terminus. There's no need for anyone to stay on the train . . . Do you hear the night wind? The voice from the other side of fear and madness? That is the terminus . . . without a ticket . . . Good night, friend, *nos da*!

(We hear the compartment door open and close with a bang. The Traveller exits upstage left under cover of the darkness. The Guard switches on the compartment light and closes the window – cutting off the sound of the hymn; the train sound is brought down simultaneously. The Guard looks about him for a moment, then leaves the compartment and exits upstage right along the corridor.)

GUARD: *Tocynnau!* Tickets!

(The train sound comes up as the light fades to black in the empty compartment.)

Appendix

THE PRONUNCIATION OF WELSH

The Welsh alphabet uses 28 letters: a, b, c, ch, d, dd, e, f, ff, g, ng, h, i, l, ll, m, n, o, p, ph, r, rh, s, t, th, u, w, y.

In general, the consonants represent the same sound-values as in English spelling, with these exceptions:

c: always the sound in 'cat', never the sound in 'cease'.

ch: as in the Scottish word 'loch'.

dd: the sound represented by the 'the' in 'breathe'; Welsh uses 'th' only for the sound in 'breath'.

f: as in 'of'.

ff: as in 'off'.

g: always the sound in 'give', never the sound in 'germ'.

ll: there is no equivalent sound in English; the usual advice is to pronounce 'tl' rapidly as if it were a single sound, or to put the tip of the tongue on the roof of the mouth and hiss.

ph: as in 'physic'.

r: the sound is always trilled.

rh: the trilled 'r' followed by aspiration.

s: always the sound in 'sea', never the sound in 'does'. 'si' is used for the sound represented in English spelling by 'sh'; English 'shop' becomes Welsh 'siop'.

Welsh letters stand always for pure vowel-sounds, never as in English spelling for diphthongs. The vowels can be long or short; a circumflex accent is sometimes used to distinguish the long vowel.

a: the vowel-sounds in 'father' and (American) 'hot'.

e: the vowel-sounds in 'pale' and 'pet'.

i: the vowel-sounds in 'green' and 'grin'. The letter is also used for the consonantal sound represented in English spelling by 'y'; English 'yard' becomes Welsh 'iard'.

o: the vowel-sounds in 'roll' and (British) 'hot'.

u: pronounced like the Welsh 'i'. Never used as in English spelling.

w: the vowel-sounds in 'tool' and 'took'. English 'fool' becomes Welsh 'ffŵl'. The letter is also used consonantally as in English, 'dwelling', 'Gwen'.

y: in most monosyllables and in final syllables pronounced like the Welsh 'i'; in other syllables it stands for the vowel sound in 'up', and this is also its sound in a few monosyllables like 'y' and 'yr'.

The following diphthongs are used in Welsh; the chief vowel comes first:

ae, ai, au: the diphthong sound in 'write'.

ei, eu, ey: 'uh-ee'.

aw: the diphthong sound in 'prowl'.

ew: the short Welsh 'e' followed by 'oo'.

iw, yw: 'ee-oo'.

wy: 'oo-ee'.

oe, oi, ou: the sound in 'oil'.

The accent in Welsh is placed, with few exceptions, on the penult: Llýwarch, Llywélyn.